Mikhail Kuzmin
Selected Writings

Portrait of Mikhail Kuzmin (1924) by photographer Moisei Nappelbaum. Courtesy of Ilya Rudiak.

Mikhail Kuzmin
Selected Writings

Translated from Russian, Edited, Annotated,
and with an Introduction

by Michael A. Green and Stanislav A. Shvabrin

Lewisburg
Bucknell University Press

Associated University Presses
2010 Eastpark Boulevard
Cranbury, NJ 08512

The paper used in this publication meets the requirements of the
American National Standards for Permanence of Paper for Printed
Library Materials Z39.48-1984.

Library of Congress Cataloging-in-Publication Data

Kuzmin, M. A. (Mikhail Alekseevich), 1872–1936.
    [Selections. English. 2005]
    Selected writings / Mikhail Kuzmin ; translated from Russian, edited,
annotated, and with an introduction by Michael A. Green and Stanislav
A. Shvabrin.
        p.   cm.
    Includes bibliographical references.
    ISBN 0-8387-5601-8 (alk. paper)
    1. Kuzmin, M. A. (Mikhail Alekseevich), 1872–1936—Translations into
English.   I. Green, Michael A., 1937– .II. Shvabrin, Stanislav.   III.
Title.
PG3467.K93A244   2005
891.71′3—dc22   2004021853

Contents

Theater

Prose

Literary Manifestoes

Acknowledgments

THE EDITORS AND TRANSLATORS OF THIS COLLECTION WISH TO EX-
press their gratitude to the following scholars whose re-
search on Kuzmin has been of great help to them:
John A. Barnstead, N. A. Bogomolov, Marie-Louise Bott,
George Cheron, A. N. Gorbunov, Neil Granoien, Judith E.
Kalb, A. V. Lavrov, John E. Malmstad, Vladimir Markov,
G. A. Morev, Irina Paperno, Gennady Shmakov, S. V. Shumik-
hin, R. D. Timenchik, A. G. Timofeyev, V. N. Toporov, T. V.
Tsiv'yan.

Kuzmin's posthumous indebtedness to the late Carl R.
Proffer, together with Ellendea Proffer, editors of Ardis Pub-
lishers, can hardly be exaggerated.

We would also like to thank Jerome H. Katsell for a careful
reading of our manuscript that resulted in much sound advice. We appreciate the critiques of our work provided by
anonymous reviewers for Bucknell University Press.

We are grateful to the late Vera T. Reck for sharing with us
her magnificent collection of Kuzminiana.

The practical assistance provided by the Academic Senate
Council on Research, Computing and Library Resources,
University of California at Irvine helped to bring this project
to completion.

Mikhail Kuzmin

Many russian writers have called forth differing responses from their contemporaries, but there are few, if any, who can rival Mikhail Kuzmin in the number of utterly contradictory estimates his work has received. His poetry aroused the enthusiasm of connoisseurs, while his prose gave rise to scandal and passionate dispute. Many aspects of Kuzmin—poet, dramatist, novelist and short story writer, performer, libertine and dandy—induced reactions that ranged from rapture and delight to loathing; his appearance, unconventional manner and—not least—a sexual orientation he made no attempt to conceal, could not but disturb. Here are a few reactions:

> Kuzmin the pederast, with his half-barren cranium and graveyard face painted like the corpse of a prostitute
>
> (Ivan Bunin)

> [In Kuzmin] there was no affectation: there was the inborn elegance of an alien species, a special elegance of frame; there was the tea-drinker's flyaway little finger—so drank Lafayette, liberator of America, in the eighteenth century; so drank from a pewter mug André Chénier, most courageous of poets, in the *Conciergerie*; apart from a personal elegance of frame there was a physical tradition, a physical inheritance, a "mannerism"—something inborn.
>
> (Marina Tsvetayeva)

> For Kuzmin art is everything.
>
> (Aleksei Remizov)

Kuzmin is an emblematic figure of Russian civilization at the beginning of the twentieth century. He is one of the most vivid and vibrant personalities of Russian Modernism; he was fated to join the cohort of underground "makers" of the Soviet period, a writer who has had to wait decades for a rediscovery that is still in process (at least outside Russia).

Much has changed since the appearance in 1972 of the first

13

translation into English of a selection of Kuzmin's work.[1] Since then, great interest has developed in Kuzmin: he is widely published in Russia; excellent biographies have come out in English as well as in Russian.[2] It is time for a new collection of Kuzmin's work.

I.

Mikhail Alekseyevich Kuzmin was born October 6, 1872, in Yaroslavl, an ancient city on the Volga. A scion of the provincial gentry, Kuzmin was zealous throughout his life in maintaining the aristocratic absence of a "soft sign" in the writing of his family name that effectively differentiated him from less genteel but far more numerous bearers of an otherwise identical name. "My Forebears," the opening poem of Kuzmin's debut collection Nets, makes a partial record of the ancestors but for whom he would not have made an appearance in this world, naming glittering mariners as well as matrons of the imperial backwaters; among them are a celebrated French actor of his day who settled in St. Petersburg and aspiring actresses who vanished leaving scarcely a trace. The poet feels an obligation to present a personal account of generations long gone, finding his own voice in a warm acceptance of his family's past. The unease, protest and revolt of an unsettled period are alien to Kuzmin, although his childhood and adolescence were certainly not free of dissension.

The poet's father was Aleksei Alekseyevich Kuzmin (1812–1886), a retired naval officer; his mother, Nadezhda Dmitriyevna, née Fyodorova (1834–1904), was the daughter of an actress. The atmosphere of the household was by no means tranquil: as the poet was to recall, both his parents were of an independent disposition, not inclined to compromise. A late child, Kuzmin grew up surrounded by female relatives, immersed in a world of his own; an interest in the arts awakened early—music captivated him first—together with the creative impulse.

A document that sheds light on the early—pre-St. Petersburg, pre-literary—period of the poet's life is the autobiographical fragment entitled Histoire édifiante de mes commencements.[3] The piece, written as if by a casual observer, conveys an impression of a thin-skinned, sensitive individual not altogether devoid of narcissism. The *Histoire édifiante*, written in 1906, serves as prologue to the diary kept by Kuzmin until the end of his life—a unique chronicle, packed with information about the author's daily round and the ways of literary Petersburg/Petrograd/Leningrad of the first third of the twentieth century.

In 1884 the Kuzmins left Saratov, where they had moved from Yaroslavl when the future poet was but one and a half years of age, to settle in St. Petersburg. Entry into the life of the capital was far from easy for a provincial youngster short on funds. Although Kuzmin did not much care for the school he had to attend, it was here that he encountered a remarkable personality who in many ways foreordained the pattern of his life: in 1886 Georgii Chicherin ("Yusha" to relatives and friends) became one of Kuzmin's fellow students in the city's Eighth Gymnasium. The future People's Commissar for Foreign Affairs in the Bolshevik administration, Georgii Vasil'yevich Chicherin (1872–1936, dates by a quirk of fate identical to Kuzmin's own), was the offspring of a wealthy aristocratic family; he knew several languages and had received domestic instruction in music and the arts. Chicherin's influence on Kuzmin was a positive one: it was surely through Chicherin that his best friend learned to conceive of himself as a creative force, of art as his vocation. Particularly significant in Kuzmin's development was the fact that Chicherin shared a predilection directed, as the future poet was now beginning to understand, toward his own sex.

The correspondence between Chicherin and Kuzmin impresses with the breadth of these young men's cultural interests (Chicherin had not been reluctant to assume the role of mentor): they discuss Mozart, the German romantics, Goldoni and Gozzi, Gnosticism and the exotic stylizations of Pierre Louÿs—with such baggage was Kuzmin later to enter the literary world.[4] Before the artist in Kuzmin took shape, he had become a man of the Art Nouveau era, sensitive to European cultural trends of the day, intent on initiating a *frisson nouveau* in his native land.

On completing the gymnasium, rather than proceeding to university, as would have been expected of a young man of his circumstances, Kuzmin chose to study music, and in the summer of 1891 successfully passed the entrance exams for the St. Petersburg Conservatoire (Chicherin, who dreamed of a diplomatic career, chose the more conventional path).

Among Kuzmin's instructors at the Conservatoire were Nikolai Rimsky-Korsakov and Anatolii Lyadov. Resolved to become a composer, Kuzmin began work on an opera *Helen*, based on motifs from Leconte de Lisle. However, Kuzmin grew disillusioned with the Conservatoire and came to doubt his gift as a composer; he experienced a powerful infatuation with a mysterious "Prince Georges"; there was an attempted suicide, a reconciliation with his mother, to whom he confided his secret.

In May of 1895 Kuzmin set off, according to the diary, in the company of "Prince Georges," on a journey to Egypt and the Near East, during which he discovered a city that was to enchant his imagination—Alexandria. "Prince Georges" disappeared from Kuzmin's life as unexpectedly as he had entered it: according to the poet, his lover died suddenly in Vienna while visiting an aunt (it should be recorded that Kuzmin's biographers have not been able to offer any identification of "Prince Georges").

Striving to come to terms with himself and find a direction for his life, Kuzmin broke with the Conservatoire; we know that he went through a period of religious devotion. On the brink of a nervous breakdown, he had to undergo treatment for a mental disorder. A journey to Italy in the spring and summer of 1897 brought some assuagement. In Rome, however, Kuzmin found a new passion, this time for a hotel "lift-boy." A concerned Chicherin sought to end the affair through the intervention of Canon Mori, a respected elderly cleric whose dream was to set Kuzmin on the path of salvation by converting him to Catholicism. Rome, Florence—Italy—would be lodged forever in the poet's heart, and would find their place in his writings.

On his return to Russia, Kuzmin, having resisted conversion to Catholicism but unsatisfied with Orthodoxy, turned to the teachings of the Old Believers—a conservative branch of Russian Orthodoxy, which had broken with the "official" Church and repudiated its role in the empire's state apparatus. By now an adept in the music, languages and literatures of Western Europe, he discovered the culture, the writings and music of ancient Russia. Gradually Kuzmin assumed the visage that was to be uniquely his own, reconciling in himself Alexandria and the sanctuaries of the Old Believers, Mozart and the litany of the Russian Church. Letters of the 1890s addressed to Chicherin had contained Kuzmin's earliest experimentation with verse; now he turned to poetry anew, in 1903–4 trying his hand at an adaptation of the spiritual Russian folksong. Writing was to become central to Kuzmin's life, although he was never entirely to abandon music. It was this interest that led him to participate in the "Evenings of Contemporary Music" arranged by a group of artistically inclined denizens of St. Petersburg connected with the World of Art association. It was they who were responsible for the genesis of the magazine of the same name and the movement identified with Serge Diaghilev, Alexandre Benois, Leon Bakst, Konstantin Somov—a pleiad of original artists, composers, choreographers and dancers.

Kuzmin made his literary debut in *The Green Miscellany of Verse and Prose*, a collection published at the expense of the family of one of its contributors. Kuzmin's sonnets and an ambitious, if derivative, drama-cum-libretto entitled *History of the Knight d'Alessio* caught the attention of Valerii Yakovlevich Bryusov (1873–1924)—a leading Symbolist and editor of the influential Moscow-based literary monthly *Libra*. It was in this journal that selections from Kuzmin's poetry began to appear, among them the prelude to the cycle "This Summer's Love" that marked the entrance into Russian letters of a new voice that spoke of a subject barely mentionable at that time—homosexual love. *Libra* was soon to devote an entire issue (November, 1906) to Kuzmin's novel *Wings*, a tale of the spiritual and sexual self-discovery of its protagonist, Ivan Smurov—one that undoubtedly reflects the author's own difficult path to self-acceptance.[5]

In the second decade of the last century Kuzmin began to publish in the St. Petersburg magazine *Apollo*. It provided a bastion for a younger generation of writers uneasy with the dominance of the Symbolists, among whom were such "senior" figures as Bryusov himself, Dmitrii Merezhkovsky, Zinaida Gippius and Vyacheslav Ivanov. The editor of *Apollo*, Sergei Makovsky, was to add to the staff of his journal the future *maître* of Acmeism, a leading post-Symbolist movement—Nikolai Gumilev. And it was Gumilev who invited Kuzmin to become a contributor to *Apollo*. An article by Kuzmin, "Concerning Beautiful Clarity (Remarks on Prose)," published by *Apollo* in 1910, with its proclamation of "Clarism"—a style of calculated simplicity—as an ideal quality of the writer's art, was to become a catalyst in the development of Acmeism into an independent movement. Kuzmin himself, however, was careful to keep aloof of polemic, thus preserving both neutrality and the respect of those engaged in literary skirmishing. An uncommon talent in combination with a position "above the fray" gained for Kuzmin a special place among his contemporaries. It is worthy of note that it was Kuzmin, a recognized master, who should have written a foreword to Anna Akhmatova's first collection, *Evening* (1912), thus introducing this poet to the world.

Kuzmin belongs inalienably to the Petersburg bohemia of the twilight of empire—a dusk that, with the onset of the First World War, could not but deepen. A frequenter of the Parnassian cabaret the "Stray Dog," it was he who composed the anthem for this free association of poets and musicians, painters and dancers.

The poet's private life was not without adventure: one evanescent affair followed another, much like those that had inspired such cycles as "This Summer's Love" and "A Story Interrupted" in *Nets*, his collection of 1908. Perpetually homeless, Kuzmin made a habitat for himself in the apartment of Vyacheslav Ivanov, thus becoming a key figure in the history of the celebrated "Tower," the most interesting literary salon of the century's early years. He moved to the home of Sergei and Olga Sudeikin, with each of whom his fate had been closely intertwined. His life a muddle not improved by a chronic lack of funds, Kuzmin attempted to support himself by satisfying the undemanding readers of popular journals eager to make their pages accessible to a notorious "decadent."

Kuzmin published three verse collections before the Revolution—*Nets, Autumnal Lakes* (1912), *Clay Pigeons* (1914)—experimenting with a great variety of genre and theme. A cycle in *Nets* was to win particular acclaim—the "Alexandrian Songs" that Kuzmin would perform at the piano for a circle of friends. In these "Songs" he succeeded in evoking the mood of a city remote in time and space. Kuzmin's Alexandria enchanted the poet's contemporaries with its artless harmony and ideal freedom. Written for the most part in free verse, the "Alexandrian Songs" were unequalled in their rhythmic opulence and musicality. *Autumnal Lakes* reveals a different aspect of Kuzmin: a collection concluding with a cycle dedicated to the Holy Virgin had opened with an indecent acrostic. It was in this, his second collection, that the poet included some early experiments from an alternate line of his development—adaptations of traditional "spiritual verses." Kuzmin's third book of verse, *Clay Pigeons*, in spite of a certain flagging of inspiration, contains what is surely one of the poet's most perfect utterances, the short poem "Quietly I take my leave of you," addressed to Kuzmin's lover of the time, himself an aspiring poet, Vsevolod Knyazev. Not long after his break with Kuzmin, Knyazev, rejected by Olga Glebova-Sudeikina (wife of a former lover of Kuzmin's, the artist Sergei Sudeikin) was to put a bullet through his brain. In all likelihood, this episode provided the origin of the myth of Kuzmin as a malign force, the indifferent observer of the destruction of past lovers and friends. This myth became a commonplace, finding its most memorable embodiment in Anna Akhmatova's *Poem without a Hero*.

The Revolution that brought Kuzmin grief and deprivation also brought a renewal and ripening of his gift. Like the great majority of his compatriots, Kuzmin was doomed to a struggle for survival. However, in the years following the Revolution, Kuzmin published a number of collections: *The Guide* (1918), *Pictures under Wraps* (1920), *Echo* (1921), *Otherworldly Evenings* (1921), *Parabolas* (1923), *The Trout Breaks the Ice* (1929). It was in these collections that Kuzmin found fulfillment as a poet; it is Kuzmin's post-revolutionary work that sets his name among the great ones of twentieth century writing. Kuzmin's work of this period is endowed with a new dramatic power, springing from his conflict with surrounding reality; the collapse of a very particular world, one loved and treasured by the poet, instills this new work with the bitterness of loss. A forceful example of such a mood is to be found in a poem from *Parabolas*, "And this is one for hooligans . . ." (1922).

Most probably, the secret of this poem's effect is the capture, in all its richness, of a fleeting emotion. The simple words of a folksong evoke a sense of irredeemable catastrophe: war and revolution had changed Kuzmin's world beyond all recognition. The poetic catalogue—a device put to brilliant use in "My Forebears" of 1907—is here deployed to convey the loss of the land where the poet had once lived and loved. Kuzmin enumerates the tokens of this *paradis perdu*: names of cities, holy places, marks of abundance.

At the beginning of the twenties, Kuzmin devoted much energy to the organization of a new literary movement, one he christened "Emotionalism." For the Kuzmin who rein-

vented his poetry in the post-revolutionary years, emotion
had assumed a primary place. Rooted in the German Expressionism that had captivated Kuzmin, Emotionalism was intended to be a practical alternative to the mechanization of
art. Formalism seemed to be winning the day not only as an
analytical strategy, but also as a philosophy of artistic creation. Kuzmin's Emotionalism was to be stillborn: apart from
a handful of like-minded friends, no one was willing to sign
the "Declaration of Emotionalism," a manifesto assembled
by the poet himself (could Kuzmin have been nostalgic for
the stir caused by "Concerning Beautiful Clarity" back in
pre-revolutionary days?). The "Declaration" printed in 1923
in the journal *Abraksas* (a Greek word signifying "Creator" in
the teaching of the Gnostics) was all but ignored. The era of
boldness and enterprise in the arts was done with—not in
politics alone did a new age and a new order demand an organized and approved style. Undiscouraged, Kuzmin published a fresh manifesto solely under his own name—with
the same lack of resonance; a sensation of being out of tune
with the times overwhelmed the poet. If Emotionalism had
any consequences, they are to be sought in the later poetry
and drama of Kuzmin himself.

The poetic cycle or narrative poem "The Trout Breaks the
Ice" was written in 1927, and gave its name to the poet's last
collection, published in 1929. "Trout" has some claim to represent the summit of Kuzmin's art. A capricious maze of elu-
sive images composed of haunting moments from favorite
movies, faint hints of the psychoanalysis that was coming
into fashion, nightmares unforgotten, all go to form the in-
comparable unity of "The Trout Breaks the Ice." The poem
is infused with remembrance of things past: the affair with
Sudeikin, whose unexpected departure and marriage is in-
terwoven with another dramatic episode of the poet's biography; the writer Yurii Yurkun, Kuzmin's companion since the
time of *Clay Pigeons*, had fallen in love with the actress Olga
Arbenina-Gildebrandt. A multilayered text, "The Trout
Breaks the Ice" is a pinnacle of Russian Modernism that re-
wards with the apprehension of the complex transitory
world surrounding the poet, with the discovery of a poetic
masterpiece.

In post-revolutionary, subsequently Soviet Petrograd/Le-
ningrad, Kuzmin was at the center of a close-knit circle,
younger newcomers to which were amazed to encounter a

"living anachronism," a man from a vanished epoch.[6] Kuzmin's day-to-day life in these years is reflected in a story dating from 1922, "Underground Streams": against a backdrop of mass executions and punitive expeditions, in the midst of the new officialdom's linguistic barbarisms, the protagonist occupies himself with the acquisition and sale of rare books, preferring peace and quiet in the company of the bookworms of the former imperial capital to the phantasmagoric reality of the Bolshevik state. Through the lips of the story's heroine, Kuzmin expresses a less than plausible hope for a miracle—"underground streams" that would somehow breach the horror of existence, bringing about a transfiguration. In the story of that name the author attempts to explain to himself his inability to follow the path taken by more realistic compatriots: flight, emigration. Could Kuzmin—the aesthete, the Alexandrian—have been rendered helpless by an irrational and profound attachment to Russia that he was incapable of overcoming by force of reason?

Post-revolutionary Kuzmin enriched Russian poetry with a number of exceptional creations unpublishable during his lifetime (in the first edition of the collection *The Trout Breaks the Ice*, a poem hinting at Bolshevik mass executions was replaced by rows of dots). The cycle "Thrall" of 1919, the poems "December frosts the rosy sky" of 1920, "No governor's lady with officer conversing" of 1924, "Settlers" of 1927—all of which could be published only many years after Kuzmin's death—revealed him to be a poet who had undergone a remarkable creative evolution. Alas, his late work proved the most vulnerable to vicissitude: much of Kuzmin's post-revolutionary writing disappeared into secret service archives, or was scattered and lost during the blockade of Leningrad.

In 1929 Kuzmin put the finishing touches to a longstanding design, bringing to completion a monumental drama, *The Death of Nero*, the inspiration for which had come to him in 1924, during the funeral of Vladimir Lenin. Kuzmin's *Death of Nero* is a complex work rich in sub-texts, blasphemously bold historical parallels, chronological intertwinings, and play of hidden leitmotifs. *Nero* crowns Kuzmin's long career as a dramatist, demonstrating him to be not only a penetrating thinker, but a subtle master of parody. The drama unfolds on three temporal planes: the Rome of Nero, provincial Russia at the turn of the century, Italy in the nineteen-twenties. Two men with pretensions to creativity (or might they be genuine artists?) lay alternating claim to the reader/spectator's attention. The pair are Nero himself and a dramatist, Pavel Andreyevich Lukin, who has just completed a play about Nero, the first reading of which leaves its listeners mystified. Kuzmin's drama confronts the reader with a cynically cyclical vision of progress: the Rome of Nero is transformed suddenly into the Russia of Stalin (Nero expatiates on grandiose construction projects, inquiring into the development of his newly-instituted "four-year plan"), while Pavel, Kuzmin's contemporary, is subjected to more than one truly Neronian transformation (the impoverished hanger-on turns suddenly into a titled, wealthy man who dreams of becoming a benefactor of humanity). *The Death of Nero* has had an odd fate: completed in 1929, first published in 1977, this drama has entered the new millennium with many of its mysteries unexplored, its depths unfathomed.

Kuzmin's later years were bitter and barren of hope. Gradually he was severed from his readers. For a time he was able to scrape a living from theatrical reviewing, but before long even this source of income dried up.[7] In Petersburg Kuzmin had known his moment of fame; in Petrograd came world war, revolution, civil war, the cold and starvation of "War Communism." An ideal Soviet pariah—a poet and a "pederast"—Kuzmin died in Leningrad on March the first, 1936. He was fortunate to die in a hospital: Kuzmin's companion and heir, Yurii Yurkun, was executed in 1938, having been seized during the "investigation" of a fabricated "writers' plot" that was to serve as an excuse for a bloody purge of Leningrad's intelligentsia.

II.

Two poems, separated by a goodly number of years, mark distinct stages of Kuzmin's poetic development. For many, the first of them remains to this very day Kuzmin's best-known production.

> Where shall I find a style to catch a stroll,
> Chablis on ice, a crisply toasted roll,
> The agate succulence of cherries ripe?
> "This Summer's Love" (1906), *Nets* (1908)

These lines—blasphemy for some, revelation for others—had the force of a bombshell on the Russian writing of the century's first decade. Their author, with apparent naïveté, confesses to a lack of confidence in his capacity to "find a style" in which to describe the trifles of everyday existence, thus putting into an ironically depreciative context the grandiloquence and mysticism prevalent in the poetry of the time. If a poet has difficulty in finding words to describe "a stroll," how is he to cope with transcendental verities? The poem's explosive force, however, far exceeded that of a mere ironical question. Kuzmin had revealed the ordinary world to the poetry of Russian Modernism—a genuine, if transient, "world of phenomena," which, according to Symbolist doctrine, should have been rejected in the name of a truer "world of ideas." This poem provoked a revolution in the understanding of the poetic image long usurped by Symbolism: in place of the misty primordial image, conceived by the Symbolists as being of "inexhaustible" significance ("Death," "Beauty," etc.), the deliberately down-to-earth, challengingly commonplace image of Kuzmin made its confident entry into Russian poetry. The consequences of this revolution were of undoubted benefit: into the breach hacked by Kuzmin in Symbolist aesthetics and poetics poured the fresh forces that were to shape post-Symbolist poetry—Anna Akhmatova, Nikolai Gumilev, Osip Mandelstam (to limit the list to the most potent of this pleiad). It is impossible to underestimate the service rendered by Kuzmin to those who found in themselves the strength, in the words of the critic Viktor Zhirmunsky, "to overcome Symbolism." It was probably for this reason that Kuzmin's work aroused lively interest among such poets as Velimir Khlebnikov, Vladimir Mayakovsky, Boris Pasternak, who can hardly be described as his followers.

For Kuzmin himself, the world he had discovered remained enchanting throughout the pre-revolutionary period, continuing to furnish him with the stuff of his poetry. In his earliest collections Kuzmin is the singer of the fleeting moment, of quotidian delight, of amorous adventure, of passions as tempestuous as they are ephemeral. The poet's loss of this world was a catastrophe that would change not only his outlook on life, but the very nature of his art. Anyone acquainted with Kuzmin's pre-revolutionary work would have been unlikely to have predicted his gift's survival in a cataclysm. What Kuzmin endured, though, was to transfigure him as a creative artist. The political calamity that cost the man great suffering was a blessing for the artist: Kuzmin became a tragic poet, gaining—paradoxical as it may seem—by means of deprivation a unique place in his country's literature.

The evolution whose starting point is marked by the poem cited earlier, is best illustrated by another, dating from 1921:

> Not bitter to me are need and thrall—
> Neither are hunger or destruction,
> But a chill pierces my spirit,
> In a moldy trickle swirls decay.
> "Bread," "water," "firewood": those words
> We've understood and seem to know,
> But with every passing hour forget
> Other, better words.

The admission made by Kuzmin in these lines is a remarkable one. The poet who had once cast playful doubt on his ability to do justice to "a crisply toasted roll," feels compelled to make a confession: it is only now that he has learned the true meaning of the word "bread." In essence, this is a poem replete with irony toward a former self who had fancied he understood what he was talking about in his celebrated paean to "Chablis on ice," "a toasted roll," "the agate succulence of cherries ripe." For Kuzmin, the cold and starvation of "War Communism" brought an ultimate revelation of the real content of such nouns as "bread," "water" and "firewood." Kuzmin's universe has endured a malignant transubstantiation that has reversed the Evangelical parable: before the poet's eyes wine ("Chablis on ice") turns into water, "a toasted roll" into bread, the sun's warmth into firewood. The drama of this transformation does not lie in the fact that a certain poet has perforce undergone a number of deprivations. The tragedy of Kuzmin is that the revelation of incontrovertible truths concerning the universe and human existence fails to inspire any creative upsurge, depriving him of what is most needful to a poet: "But with every passing hour [we] forget / Other, better words." This loss of "other, better words" is an essential component of the later Kuzmin's tragic pathos. Yet as an artist Kuzmin ultimately triumphed: he was one of very few who found in themselves the ability to give impeccable form to their tragedy.

Here is the concluding quatrain of this poem:

> Like pitiful excrement we lie
> In a trampled, barren field,
> And there we'll lie until the hour
> The Lord breathe into us a soul.

Another contrast emerges from the juxtaposition of these two poems: the earlier is written in the first person and has the intimate quality of chamber music. The later Kuzmin is to find new scope in his lyricism—the "we" of his post-revolutionary verse. Not that Kuzmin had earlier been able to dispense with the first person plural, but previously his "we" had often designated a pair of lovers. The "we" of the later Kuzmin (the cycle "Thrall," such poems as "December frosts the rosy sky," "Lost enchantment," the poem cited above), without losing the component of intimacy, becomes the plural voice of men and women condemned to await, in full cognizance, their inevitable end:

> December frosts the rosy sky,
> Black the rooms of this unheated house;
> And we, < . . . >
> We read the Bible and we wait.
>
> We wait. And do we know what for?
> Can it be for a redeeming hand?
>> "December frosts the rosy sky," 1920

It is not surprising that this poem circulated throughout the Russian-speaking world, capturing as it does the fate of the Russian intelligentsia in frozen Petrograd. With few exceptions, a like consciousness of doom was shared by Kuzmin's contemporaries of similar cultural background, but it was Kuzmin who found a fitting and condensed form for it.

III.

A constant theme of Kuzmin's poetry is that of captivity, dependence—unfreedom. Not by chance was his first collection entitled *Nets*, making it a statement of this very theme: a net of love, of passion, of an entanglement that may well be delicious and desired, encompassing both sensual enjoyment and spiritual harmony. In Kuzmin's early poetry such unfreedom is synonymous with love itself.

In his first collection Kuzmin succeeds in finding an adequate formula for this image. The monosyllable *plen*, rendered by "thrall" in our translation, conveys it most effectively (italics ours):

> The flute of tender Bathyllus
> *Enthralled*, subdued us,
> *Thrall* is sweet to us, *thrall* is dear . . .
> > "On Sergei Auslender's story 'The Flute of
> > Bathyllus'" (1907), *Nets*

Thrall is a leitmotif of *Nets*. With the image of "thrall" is linked another, that of the "Guide"—the ideal beloved, celestial guardian, submission to whose will brings with it bliss and contentment. At different times, the "Guide" was identified first with Victor Naumov, then with Vsevolod Knyazev (both of them officers in the imperial army, hence the frequent military associations of this image). The "Guide" was to undergo some significant transformations, becoming at last "my guiding star" ("December frosts the rosy sky . . ."). But "thrall" was destined to develop from a central image of the poet's debut collection (where it had a playful nuance), to the dominant leitmotif of Kuzmin's entire poetic output.

The cycle "Thrall" of 1919, inspired by Yurii Yurkun's imprisonment (from which, this time, he was released unharmed), elevates the image contained in its title to a new level. To begin with, the poet defines the triumph of the new political order as "enthrallment":

> Slap!
> They've thwacked our mugs with a filthy rag,
> Taken from us bread, light, warmth, meat,
> Milk, soap, paper, books,
> Clothing, boots, blankets, butter,
> Kerosene, candles, salt, sugar,
> Tobacco, matches, porridge—
> Everything.
> And they said:
> > "Live and be free!"
> > > 1, Angel of the Annunciation

Peace and freedom had been the blessings of the old life; the new order had brought imprisonment, affliction—thrall (deliverance was to come from leaders of the anti-Bolshevik resistance—Admiral Kolchak, Baron Wrangel, both of whom are named in poems unpublished in Kuzmin's lifetime). The earlier sweet and longed-for enthrallment has vanished without trace; the "nets" that entangle the poet are different. Awareness of the impossibility of escape leads Kuzmin to a further logical step in the evolution of this image: life itself has become captivity, thrall; hope of release is now linked solely with death. The time that the "we" of "December frosts the rosy sky" are attempting to kill by reading the Bible in their exile

> No, we are only exiles,
> Only exiles, my poor love . . .

turns out to be the expectation of death.

A poem of 1927, "Settlers," develops the image of exile, thrall, bringing to the reader's mind a comparison of the lot of English settlers in America with that of the dwellers of imperial St. Petersburg who find themselves in Soviet Leningrad:

> An alien sun beyond an alien swamp
> Roosts frantically upon its perch.
> And tomorrow autocratically will rise anew
> Not punishing, not conferring favor.

The poet comes to a comprehension of an alien and hateful world that has sprung up around him, where all he has left are memories of a distant ancestral home to which there can be no return:

> Better to sleep till midday, Molly—
> Perhaps you'll dream of the bank of the Thames,
> And the ivy-covered house where you were born.

Kuzmin's "Settlers" bears witness to the mastery of unrhymed verse the poet has attained. What may seem novel in the later Kuzmin proves, on examination, to be solidly founded on devices, motifs and themes refined over a long creative career. The constant refinement of the alliteration so characteristic of Kuzmin's poetry reaches its peak in the musicality of "December frosts the rosy sky." Kuzmin had drawn on spiritual folk poetry in his earliest attempts to express himself in verse: therefrom came the "Spiritual Verses" of *Autumnal Lakes*.[8] He returned to this source in a poem of November 1924, "No governor's lady with officer conversing," which is a revival of "spiritual verses" in full accord with the tradition of folk poetry. The genre here is that of the "vision," in which the Holy Virgin, in the presence of the Archangel Michael, decides the fate of a Russia that has rejected God, Tsar and even its own name. The Holy Virgin and the Archangel Michael are often encountered in Kuzmin's writings (see such cycles as "Spiritual Verses," "Feasts of the Most Holy Mother of God" in *Autumnal Lakes*; the Archangel Michael, Kuzmin's patron saint, is to be met elsewhere in his poetry). "No governor's lady with officer conversing," written in 1924, bears some resemblance to one of the "Spiritual Verses" of 1904, "The Virgin Visits Hell." But the contrast between these two poems is significant: if the earlier tells of the Virgin's compassion (it is she who begs of her son respite for sinners tormented in hell), the judgment she voices in the later poem is exactly the reverse—Virgin calls upon Archangel to chastise the servants of the new regime:

> I am a woman. I feel sorry even for a villain.
> But these I don't consider human.
> Their very selves they have rejected,
> Renouncing their immortal souls.
> To you I hand them over. Be just.

IV.

However many-sided this writer's gift, his work must be perceived as a totality. With such a guiding principle, the translators and editors of the following selection of Kuzmin's writings have aimed to give the reader not only some conception of the richness of this writer's legacy, but also an idea of the surprising logic of his development.

Without Kuzmin, the picture of Russia in the twentieth century would be incomplete, and it is this lacuna that our collection aims to fill. With the restoration of the rights of Mikhail Kuzmin, it may be claimed that a step has been taken toward a juster presentation of the history of Russian literature.

Kuzmin's underground streams have taken long to break out into the light of day, but it may be that the poet's hopes will not, after all, prove implausible.

Mikhail Kuzmin
Selected Writings

Poetry

My Forebears

Seafarers of ancient pedigree,
enamored of distant horizons,
quaffing wine in dusky ports of call,
pert foreign lasses in their arms;
coxcombs of the eighteen-thirties,
modeling themselves on d'Orsay and Brummel,
bringing to the dandy's pose
all the naïveté of an adolescent race;
be-starred, imposing generals—
the charming beaux of yesteryear—
recounting droll yarns over a glass of rum
(always the same old yarns);
delightful actors of no great talent,
importing the style of an alien land,
performing *Mahomet* in Russia,
innocent Voltaireans to their dying day;
and you, damsels in bandeaux,
who play with such feeling the *valses* of Marcailhou,
embroidering pouches with beads
for suitors on distant campaigns,
partaking of the sacrament in household chapels,
telling fortunes by cards;
wise and thrifty ladies of the manor,
preening yourselves on well-stocked larders,
skilled in forgiving, in fostering friendships,
and putting a full stop,
mocking and pious at once,
rising before dawn in winter;
drama school blossoms, exquisitely foolish,
dedicated to the dance from childhood,
tenderhearted wantons,
immaculate profligates,
bankrupting a husband for a dress,
allotting your children half an hour per day;
yet further off, yet more remote—boondocks gentry,
obdurate boyars they might be called,
Frenchmen who fled the revolution
not managing quite to mount the guillotine—

all of you, every one of you—
having kept silence age-long,
in hundreds of voices call out now,
dead and buried, but alive
in me: the last of the lot, impoverished,
but gifted with a tongue for you,
and every drop of blood in me
is close to you,
feels you, loves you;
so here you are, all of you:
charming and silly and touching and dear;
for your silent blessing
you are blessed by me.

May, 1907

This Summer's Love

for Pavel Maslov

1.

Where shall I find a style to catch a stroll,
Chablis on ice, a crisply toasted roll,
The agate succulence of cherries ripe?
The sunset's far, the ocean's splashing cool
Can offer solace to a sunburnt nape.

The sly come-hither of your velvet gaze
Is like the darling prattle in some plays,
Like the capricious pen of Marivaux.
Your Pierrot nose, your mouth's befuddling gash
Put my head in a whirl, like Mozart's "Figaro."

Spirit of aery and delicious trifles,
Of a night of love that pampers us and stifles,
Of the weightless joy of life's unthinking mirth!
Ah I am true, remote from docile miracles,
To your flowers and none other, O blithe earth!

2.

Serpent eyes and coilings serpentine,
Play of light on motley tissues,
Unexampled sultry motions . . .
From the bashful to the shameless,
Kisses of all shades and scope,
Heady scent of ashen roses . . .

Hot embraces, heart's wild beating,
Of snakelike arms the intertwinings,
Of limbs the practiced palpitations,
Of lips on flesh the practiced ardor,
Buoyancy of a promised tryst
And leave-taking across the threshold.

3.

O lips kissed by so many,
By so many other lips.
You pierce the heart with bitter arrows,
With bitter arrows, hundreds of them.

Blossom you will in confident smiles,
Like radiant burgeoning of bushes in springtime,
Recalling caresses of delicate fingers,
Of fingers delicate and cherished.

Pilgrim or impudent desperado—
Not a single kiss is kept at bay.
Be he Antinous or be he vile Thersites,
Each man will find a fitting fortune.

A kiss that's pressed upon your flesh
Sets on that flesh a lasting mark:
Who of loved lips takes communion
Is rendered kith and kin of every lover past.

Prayerful gaze on icon fixed
Is held there fast with powerful fetters:
The ancient countenance, prayer-glorified
With those fetters binds the worshiper.

Thus do you walk in perilous places,
In perilous and holy places—
O lips kissed by so many,
By so many other lips.

4.

We washed and then got dressed,
After the night we kissed each other,
After the caress-filled night.
Using the lilac tea service,
As if with a brother, as if with a guest,
We drank tea, keeping on our masks.

They smiled, those masks of ours,
And our glances did not meet
And our lips said not a word.

We sang from *Faust*, playing the piano,
As if we had not known that night;
We are not they, those night ones, we.

5.

A parched rose drooped in doleful fashion
From a basket left behind by someone,
And they sang for us that aria of Rosina:
"Io sono docile, io sono rispettosa."

Candles burned, a warm and drowsiness—
Diffusing rain dripped scarcely heeded from the trees,
Pesaro's swan, voluptuous and stately,
With gaiety capped his briefest bar.

Friends' tales of bygone wanderings,
Disputes fine-pointed where the mind takes wing.
But all this while in expectation vain
My tender friend in solitude roams the garden.

Ah radiant are the kisses of Mozartian tones,
Like distances remote of Raphael's "Parnassus,"
Yet they can't make me forget the meeting
I haven't had with you since four o'clock.

6.

Why does the newly risen moon grow roseate
And the wind, filled with warm sweetness, breathe?
And the skiff seem mindless of the snakeskinned surge
When my spirit is locked in fasting for your sake?

When your eye I do not eye,
I am seared by memories of nights of love—
The enchantment of dear, delicious trifles
Keeps jealous watch although I am at rest:

The calm look of the river's distant windings,
The rare light in an unsleeping window,
The broken threads of cloud soft-gleaming
Won't drive away my sad and tender thoughts

Of other gardens' shadowy paths—
And dawn's uncertain glimmering . . .
The lanterns glitter with a final flame . . .
A sprightly verve love's ventures have . . .

The soul flies to abandoned pleasures,
The mildest poisons have a potent suture;
It's not for summer's meek and simple herbs
To drown the fragrance of the rose.

7.

I cannot sleep: my spirit pines,
My head is going round and round
And empty is my bed—
Where are the shoulders, where the arms,
Where the broken sentences
And the lips that I adore? . . .

The sheet had twisted about me,
My sweltering body burned,
Night was black against the pane . . .
My heart is pounding, dry my hands.
To drive away love's longing
I have no strength, I am too weak . . .

We held each other tight, we kissed,
Each with the other intertwined
Like paladin and serpent . . .
The smell of mint came drifting in,
The pillow's rumpled quite,
And I'm alone, I'm all alone.

8.

Every evening I look down from the steep
At the smooth waters glittering afar;
I note which steamer's going past:
The Kamensk one, the Volga one, or the Lyubim one.
The sun is very close to setting,
And always I keep steady watch to see
If there's a star above the steamer's wheel—
That's when it passes my vantage point.
If no star's visible—must be a mail-boat,

Could be bringing letters with my address.
I rush down to the landing stage,
Where stands the mail-coach, ready and waiting.
O ye leather bags with massive locks,
How ponderous you are, how elephantine!
And surely there are letters from beings dear to me,
Letters written with their own dear hands?
So beats my heart, so sweetly does it ache
While I stand waiting at the mailman's back:
Will there be a letter for me or won't there?
And this delectable riddle tortures me.
And O, the mountain road is star-decked now.
To be alone, and without a letter!
The road is a direct one.
Here and there light burns, houses nestle in their gardens.
It's here at last, a letter from my friend:
"I'm always calling you to mind,
No matter who I'm with, be it this or that one."
Nothing to be done—exactly the way he is
I love him and accept him.
Steamers will pull out, borne by the waves,
And I'll gaze sadly after them—
O my friends, my dear ones,
When shall I set eyes on you again?

9.

I'm sitting reading fairy tales and true ones,
Looking at portraits of the dead in ancient volumes,
They say, the portraits of the dead in ancient volumes:
"You've been forgotten, you've been forgotten . . ."

—What can I do about it if I've been forgotten,
What's to be done about it, ancient portraits?—
That's what I'm asking you, ancient portraits,
Will threats, oaths or entreaties do me any good?

"You too will forget the shoulders you have kissed,
Be then like us, be a portrait ancient and enamoured:
You'd make a good enamoured portrait
With look that's languishing, uttering no word."

—Of measureless love I am drooping and dying!
Can you not see that, O portraits I treasure?—

"We see it, we see it," the portraits assured me,
"What are you—a lover who's faithful and true?"

Thus sat I reading fairy tales and true ones,
Looking at portraits of the dead in ancient volumes.
And I wasn't sorry when the portraits whispered:
"You've been forgotten, you've been forgotten."

10.

I am so weary, tired to death.
What yesterday still held my dreams
Has suddenly lost all sense and worth.
I cannot escape the thrall
Of certain shoulders, certain eyes,
Of certain passionate and tender trysts.

Like a wounded man in the grass I lie,
Gazing at the infant moon.
The changing of the long-drawn hours
Of unchanging love brings no betrayal.
How alien, how vacant is the world to me
If I do not glimpse the lips I love!

O gladness of the heart, O love,
When again shall I behold you?
When again with entrancing poison
Shall your cunning gaze imbue me,
And tenderness of hands I know
Restore to me my faithful friend?

I lie here haunted by a single thought:
I see the distant town, I see our house,
I see the garden where the gymnasts leap,
To which we made our way so often.
O house I love! O threshold dear!
I'm tired to death, I am so weary ...

11.

No matter that drizzle has soaked my clothes:
It has brought with it a precious hope.

Soon I'll be leaving, be leaving this town,
This dreary picture no more shall I see.

I count remaining days and hours,
No longer do I write or go for walks or read.

I'll soon be on my way—no point in settling down.
Tomorrow, tomorrow morning I'll get the packing done!

Long road ahead, unbearable you are and longed-for,
Day of departure, you are so remote, so strange!

I'm eager to be off, yet filled with fear and trembling,
I dare not believe our tender meeting's near.

Villages, mountains, rivers—they'll all go flashing by,
Never will I perhaps set eyes on them again.

And I don't see anything, know nothing—
Dreaming only of the lips and eyes I love.

The tenderness I'll hoard in separation
Will make our kiss of greeting sweeter still.

So I'm glad the drizzle has soaked my clothes:
It has brought with it a precious hope.

12.

The chugging steamer's in a hurry,
Its measured chugging seems to say:
"Be calm, my friend, for very soon
You'll glimpse the sweetness of that gaze,
From tedious torments you'll find rest
In caresses of the hands you knew."

My sleep's uneasy; light repose
Brings me dreams of my dearest friend:
Now leavetaking, now greeting clasps,
A fresh encounter, more embraces.
So many days of parting
Add passion to the hour of love.

Beneath a window now I'm lying,
And scarcely bothering to take a peek.
The coastline slips by playfully,
As if it were a melody of Mozart,
And through the clefts of lustrous cloud
A ray of sunlight softly glows.

I'm like one drunk with happiness.
Everyone is dear to me: captain,
And passenger, and matelot;
Casual roadway questioning is all
I fear: I do not wish my mind
To lose its clarity of thought.

The chugging steamer's in a hurry,
Its measured chugging seems to say:
"Be calm, my friend, for very soon
You'll glimpse the sweetness of that gaze,
From tedious torments you'll find rest
In caresses of the hands you knew."

June—August 1906

Alexandrian Songs

for Nikolai Feofilaktov

I. Prelude

1.

Like a mother's lullaby
over her baby's cradle,
like a mountain echo
at daybreak answering the shepherd's pipe,
like the remote surge
of my native sea, long unbeheld,
your name rings in my ears,
thrice-blessed:
          Alexandria!

Like the hesitant whispering,
in the oak's deep shade, of love's confessions,
like the mysterious murmur
of the shadowy sacred groves,
like the tambourine of great Cybele,
bringing to mind far thunder and the moan of doves,
your name rings in my ears,
thrice-sapient:
          Alexandria!

Like the sound of a trumpet before battle,
the scream of eagles over the abyss,
the rushing wings of Nike in flight,
your name rings in my ears,
thrice-mighty:
          Alexandria!

2.

When I hear the word "Alexandria,"
I see the white walls of a house,
a little garden with a clump of stock,

the pale sunlight of an autumn evening,
and I hear the sound of distant flutes.

When I hear the word "Alexandria,"
I see the stars over the quieting town,
drunken sailors in shady hangouts,
a dancing girl whirling in the "wasp,"
and I hear the jingle of a tambourine, the shouts of a quarrel.

When I hear the word "Alexandria,"
I see a faded crimson sunset over a sea of green,
I see the fleeced and winking stars
and a pair of clear grey eyes beneath thick brows—
eyes I see
even when I do not hear the word "Alexandria."

3.

The twilight enshrouding the warm sea at evening,
the beacons that flame to the darkening heavens,
the drift of verbena when feasting is done with,
the freshness of dawn after nights spent unsleeping,
the shouting and laughter of womenfolk bathing,
the peacocks of Juno that walk in her temple,
the vendors of violets, pomegranates and lemons,
the moaning of doves and the dazzle of sunlight—
O when shall I see you, adorable city?

II. Love

1.

When it was I first encountered you
poor memory cannot tell me:
was it morning, or in the afternoon,
evening, perhaps, or late at night?
I remember only the wan cheeks,
the grey eyes beneath dark brows
and the deep-blue collar at the swarthy throat,
and all this seems to come to me from childhood,
although I am older than you, older by many years.

2.

Were you apprenticed to a fortune teller?—
My heart lies open to you,

you can divine my every thought,
my deepest meditations are not hidden from you;
but knowing this, you know but little,
few words are needed for the telling of it,
no crystal ball or glowing brazier:
my heart, my thoughts, my deepest meditations
are filled with voices endlessly repeating:
"I love you, and my love shall have no ending!"

3.

At noon I must have been conceived,
at noon I must have come into the world,
and from my childhood I have loved
the beaming radiance of the sun.
One day I looked into your eyes
and I became indifferent to the sun:
why should I adore a single sun
now that two of them are mine?

4.

People see gardens and houses
and sea crimson with sunset,
people see gulls skimming the waves,
and women on flat roofs,
people see warriors in armor
and pie-sellers in the town square,
people see sun and stars,
brooks and bright rivers,
but I see only
grey eyes beneath dark brows,
the touch of pallor in the swarthy cheeks,
the form of matchless grace—
thus do the eyes of lovers see
no more than the wise heart wills.

5.

Leaving my house in the morning,
I look up at the sun and think:
"How like my love
when he bathes in the river,
or gazes at the distant vegetable plots!"

And when in the heat of noon I gaze
at the same burning sun,
again you come into my mind, my dearest one:
"How like my love
when he rides through the crowded streets!"
And when I look upon soft sunsets,
it is to you that memory returns,
drowsing, wan from our caresses,
your drooping eyelids shadowed deep.

6.

Not for nothing did we read the theologians
and studied the rhetoricians not in vain,
for every word we have a definition
and can interpret all things seven different ways.
In your body I can locate the four virtues,
and, needless to say, the seven sins;
nor am I backward in tasting these delights;
but of all words one is changeless:
when, gazing deep into your grey eyes,
I say, "I love you"—the most ingenious rhetorician
will understand only, "I love you"—nothing more.

7.

Were I a general of olden times,
I would subdue the Ethiops and the Persians,
I would dethrone Pharaoh,
I would build myself a pyramid
higher than Cheops',
and I would become
more glorious than any man in Egypt.

Were I nimble thief,
I would rob the tomb of Menkaure,
I would sell the gems to the Jews of Alexandria,
I would buy up land and mills,
and I would become
richer than any man in Egypt.

Were I a second Antinous—
he who drowned in the sacred Nile—
I would drive all men mad with my beauty,

temples would be raised to me while I yet lived,
and I would become
more powerful than any man in Egypt.

Were I a sage steeped in wisdom,
I would squander all my wealth,
I would shun office and occupation,
I would guard other men's orchards,
and I would become
freer than any man in Egypt.

Were I your lowliest slave,
I would sit in a dungeon
and once a year or once in two years
I would glimpse the golden tracery of your sandals
when you chanced to walk by the prison house,
and I would become
happier than any man in Egypt.

III. She

1.

Four of us there were, sisters, four of us,
each of us loved, but each had a different "because":
the first because her father and mother had ordered her to,
the second because her lover possessed great riches,
the third because her lover was a famous artist,
but I loved because I fell in love.

Four of us there were, sisters, four of us,
each of us had a wish, but each wished for something
    different:
the first to raise children and cook porridge,
the second to put on a new dress every day,
the third to have everyone talking about her,
but I wished to love and to be loved.

Four of us there were, sisters, four of us,
each of us ceased to love, but each for a different reason:
the first because her husband died,
the second because her friend went bankrupt,
the third because the artist left her,

but I ceased to love because I ceased to love.
Four of us there were, sisters, four of us,
or were there perhaps not four of us, but five?

2.

In spring the poplar renews its leaves,
in spring Adonis returns
from the kingdom of the dead ...
and you are leaving me in spring, my dearest one?
In spring everyone will be at the seaside
sailing, or riding swift horses
through the parks on the edge of town ...
But who's to sail with me in a skimming skiff?

In spring everyone will put their finery on
and stroll in couples to the flowery fields ...
and you expect me to sit at home?

3.

Today's a holiday:
the bushes are all in bloom,
the currants have ripened
and the lotus floats like a beehive on the pond!
If you like,
we'll race each other
along the path bordered with yellow roses
to the lake where goldfish swim.
If you like,
we'll go to the summerhouse,
and sweet drinks will be brought to us,
pies and nuts;
a boy will wave a fan over us
and we'll gaze
at distant fields of corn.
If you like,
I'll sing a Grecian song to the harp—
but on one condition:
you're not to fall asleep,
and you have to praise both singer and accompanist.
If you like,
I'll dance the "wasp"
all by myself on the green lawn,

for you alone.
If you like,
I'll give you currants—but not with hands:
you'll take the red berries
with your lips from mine,
and with them
kisses.
If you like, if you like,
we'll count the stars,
and whoever loses count will pay a forfeit.
Today's a holiday,
the garden's all in bloom—
come, dearest love,
and make this holiday a holiday for me!

4.

Is it not true
that pearls dissolve in vinegar,
that verbena freshens the air,
that the cooing of doves is soft to the ear?

Is it not true
that there is none to match me in all Alexandria
in luxury of sumptuous adornment,
in fine white steeds and silver harness,
in the length of my black tresses, cunningly entwined?
Is there any who has the art
to paint her eyes more skillfully than I
and to steep each finger
in a different fragrance?

Is it not true
that ever since I first set eyes on you
I see nothing else but you,
hear nothing else but you,
and long for nothing else
but to gaze into your eyes—
grey eyes beneath thick brows—
and to hear your voice?

Is it not true
that with my own hands I gave you a quince,

first having tasted of it,
sent you adroit ambassadresses of the heart,
paid your debts
(though it cost me my estate),
and for love potions
bartered my very apparel?
And is it not true
that all this was in vain?

But no matter if it be true
that pearls dissolve in vinegar,
that verbena freshens the air,
that the cooing of doves is soft to the ear—
no less shall it be true,
no less shall it be true,
that you will return my love!

5.

In imitation of Pierre Louÿs

There were four of them that month,
but only one of them did I love.
The first was utterly ruined for my sake,
every hour he sent new gifts,
selling his last mill to buy bangles
that tinkled when I danced—he stabbed himself,
but he was not the one I loved.
The second dedicated thirty elegies to me
that were read even in Rome; he wrote
that my cheeks were like the breaking dawn
and my tresses like the darkness of night—
but he was not the one I loved.

The third, ah the third was so beautiful
that his own sister strangled herself with her braid
lest she become enamoured of him;
day and night he stood outside my door,
begging me to say, "Come!"—but I kept silent,
for he was not the one I loved.
But you were not rich, you did not speak of dawns and nights,
you were not handsome,
and when at the festival of Adonis I threw you a carnation,

your clear eyes looked at me indifferently—
but you were the one I loved.

6.

Don't ask me how it happened:
my mother had gone to the market;
I swept the house clean
and sat down at the loom.
I didn't sit by the doorway, I swear I didn't,
but under the high window.
Weaving and singing I sat there;
don't ask me how it happened:
my mother had gone to the market.

Don't ask me how it happened:
the window was high up.
He must have rolled up a stone
or climbed a tree
or stood on a bench.
He said:
"I thought it was a robin,
but instead I see a Penelope.
What are you doing at home? Good day to you!"
"You're the one that's like a bird, up there in the eaves
instead of sitting in the law courts
writing those precious scrolls of yours."
"Yesterday we went sailing on the Nile—
and today my head aches."
"What's the good of it aching
if it doesn't keep you from nightly carousing?"
Don't ask me how it happened:
the window was high up.

Don't ask me how it happened:
I didn't think he could reach that far.
"What's in my mouth—can you see?"
"What should there be in your mouth?
Strong teeth and a loose tongue—
and nonsense in your head."
"There's a rose in my mouth—look."
"I don't see any rose!"
"I'll give it to you, if you like—

only you'll have to reach it yourself."
I stood on tiptoe,
I climbed onto the bench,
I climbed onto the loom (it was a strong one),
I reached out for the scarlet rose,
but the rascal said:
"With your mouth, with your mouth!
Lips must take from lips, do you hear?"
Perhaps my lips did
touch his, don't ask me.
Don't ask me how it happened:
weaving and singing I sat there;
I didn't sit by the doorway, I swear I didn't.
The window was high up:
who could reach that far?
When my mother got back, she said,
"What's come over you, Zoe?—
Instead of a narcissus, you've woven a rose!
What on earth were you thinking of?"
Don't ask me how it happened.

IV. Wisdom

1.

I asked wise men from every land:
"Why does the sun give heat?
Why does the wind blow?
Why are men born into the world?

Wise men from every land replied:
"The sun gives heat
that corn may ripen for our nourishment,
and that men may die of pestilence.
The wind blows
that ships may be brought safely to distant ports,
and that caravans may be buried in the sand.
Men are born into the world
that they may sorrowfully take leave of life
after begetting others for the grave."

"And why did the gods ordain it thus?"
"For the same reason

that they put into your head the desire
to ask idle questions."

2.

What's to be done
if the crimson of evening clouds
in the green-tinged sky
(on the left the moon has already risen,
and the great-maned star,
the harbinger of night)
fades swiftly,
utterly dissolves
before your eyes?
If our journey together along the broad way
that runs among trees, past mills
(once they were mine, but now
they are the bangles on your feet)
should end suddenly
beyond the next winding
(even though a welcoming house await us there)?
If my verse,
which I value no less
than Callimachus
(or any other great one) his,
wherein I lay away my love and all my tenderness
and winged thoughts from the gods—
the solace of my mornings,
when the sky is clear
and the scent of jasmine drifts in through the window—
tomorrow
should be forgotten like other men's?
If I shall no longer see
your face
or hear your voice?
If the wine will be drained to the lees,
the fragrance flee upon the air
and even precious stuffs
fall to dust
as the centuries pass?
Am I the less to love
these dear and fragile things
because they must decay?

3.

Eternal gods, how great is my love
for this fair world!
For the sun, the reeds,
and the gleam of the grey-green sea
through delicate acacia branches!
How I love books (they are my friends),
and the quiet of a solitary dwelling
and the distant watermelon beds
I see from my window.
How I love the crowd that throngs the square,
the shouts, the singing and the sun,
the happy laughter of boys playing ball!
The walk home after happy wanderings
with my friend (he is already far away),
late in the evening
when the first stars are out,
past inns where the lights burn early.
How I love, eternal gods,
a lucid sadness
a love with no tomorrow,
death without regret
for this sweet life,
which I love (by Dionysus I swear it)
with all my beating heart
and all my cherished flesh!

4.

Sweet is it to die
to the whistle of arrows and lances
on the field of battle,
when the trumpet sounds
and the sun stands high,
dying for the glory of the fatherland
and hearing on every side:
"Hero, farewell!"
Sweet is it to die
a venerable elder
in the very house,
on the very bed
where your forefathers were born and died,
surrounded by your children,

themselves now men,
and hearing on every side:
"Father, farewell!"
But it is sweeter yet,
yet wiser,
having squandered all your wealth,
having sold your last mill
for the sake of her
you would have forgotten tomorrow,
to return from a pleasant stroll
to the house you no longer own,
to eat a leisurely supper,
and, having read the tale of Apuleius through
for the hundred and first time,
to lie in a warm, fragrant bath,
and without hearing a single farewell
to open your veins,
while through the long ceiling window
the scent of stock comes drifting in,
the sunset glitters
and the sound of flutes comes floating from afar.

5.

O sun, radiant one,
divine Ra-Helios,
it is you who bring cheer
to the hearts of emperors and heroes,
to you the sacred horses neigh,
to you they sing hymns in Heliopolis;
when you shine,
lizards crawl out onto rocks
and boys run laughing
to bathe in the Nile.
O sun, radiant one,
a pallid scribe am I,
a library recluse,
but I love you, radiant one, no less
than the sunburnt sailor
smelling of fish and brine,
and not less
than his accustomed heart
rejoices

at your royal ascent
from the ocean bed,
does my heart tremble
when, fiery still, your moted beam
comes creeping
through the narrow skylight
onto the closely written sheet
and onto my bony parchment-colored hand
tracing in cinnabar
the first letter of a hymn to you,
O sun Ra-Helios!

V. Fragments

1.

My son,
the time has come for us to part.
Long will you not see my face,
long will you not hear my voice,
and yet it seems but a short while since
that your grandfather brought you here from the desert,
and you said, gazing at me:
"Is that the god Ptah, grandad?"
Now it is you who are like the god Ptah,
and you must go forth into the world,
and you must go forth without me—
but Isis will be with you everywhere.
Do you remember our walks
along the acacia-lined paths
in the temple courtyard,
when you would talk to me of your love
and weep, your dark face growing pale?
Do you remember how from the temple walls
we would gaze at the stars
and the city would grow quiet—
near to us, and yet remote?
Of sacred mysteries I do not speak.
Tomorrow other disciples will come to me
who will not say: "Is that the god Ptah?"
because I have grown older,
and it is you who have grown to resemble the god Ptah,
but I will not forget you,

and my deepest thoughts,
my prayers,
will go with you into the wide world,
O my son.

2.

When I was led through the gardens
and through many rooms—turning now left, now right—
into a square chamber
where in the violet light that filtered through the hangings
lay
in robes stiff with jewels,
with many rings and bracelets
a woman beautiful as Hathor,
with painted eyes and tresses of jet—
I stopped in my tracks.
And she said to me:
"Well?"
But I said nothing,
and she looked at me, smiling,
and tossed me a flower from her hair,
a yellow flower.
I picked it up and raised it to my lips,
but she frowned and said:
"Did you come here,
boy,
to kiss a flower cast on the floor?"
"Yes, Empress," I murmured,
and the whole chamber rang
with the woman's silvery laughter
and with the laughter of her handmaidens;
their hands flew up as in a single motion,
their laughter came as from a single throat,
as if they were sistra at the festival of Isis
struck by the priests in unison.

3.

What a downpour!
Our sail had gotten soaking wet—
you couldn't even see that it was striped.
The rouge ran down your cheeks—
you might have been a Tyrian dyer.

Fearfully we crossed
the threshold of the charcoal-burner's hut;
our host with his scarred forehead
pushed aside his filthy brats
(covered with sores they were, their eyes inflamed),
pulled up a block for you to sit on,
flapped away the dust with his apron
and, slapping the block, said:
"How about an oatmeal cake, your honor?"
And an old black woman
was rocking a cradle and singing:
"If I were Pharaoh,
I'd buy two pears:
one I'd give to my friend,
the other I would eat myself."

4.

Once again I beheld the town where I was born
and spent my far-off youth;
I knew
that all my family and friends were gone,
I knew
that even the memory of me had vanished,
but the houses, the winding streets,
the green and distant sea
spoke to me continually
of what was unchanging—
the distant days of my childhood,
the dreams and plans of my youth,
and love that had dissolved like smoke.
A stranger utterly,
penniless,
not knowing where to lay my head,
I found myself in a remote quarter of the city
where lights shone through lowered shutters
and singing and rattle of tambourines
came from the inner rooms.
By a drawn curtain
stood a curled and pretty boy,
and when I slackened my steps, being weary,
he said to me:
"Abba,

you seem like one who has lost his way
and has no friend to turn to.
Enter in:
all things are here
to make a foreigner forget his loneliness.
Here you may find
a gay and sportive mistress,
firm-bodied and with fragrant hair."
I lingered, my mind on other things,
and, smiling, he continued:
"And if such things do not tempt you,
wanderer,
we can offer other joys
not to be despised by a wise and courageous heart."
Crossing the threshold, I cast off my sandals,
lest I should bring into a house of pleasure
the sacred dust of the desert.
Glancing at the doorkeeper,
I saw
that he was all but naked;
together we passed along the corridor
toward the welcoming tambourines.

5.

Three times I saw him face to face.
The first time was in the gardens—
I had been sent to fetch food for my comrades,
and to make the journey shorter
I took the path by the palace wing;
suddenly I caught the tremor of strings,
and being tall of stature,
I peered through the broad window and saw
him:
he was sitting alone and sad,
his slender fingers idly plucking the strings of a lyre;
a white dog
lay silent at his feet,
and only the fountain's plashing
mingled with the music.
Sensing my gaze,
he put down his lyre
and lifted his lowered face.

Magic to me his beauty
and his silence in the empty room,
in the noontide stillness.
Crossing myself, I ran away in fear,
away from the window . . .
Later, on guard duty at Lochias,
I was standing in the passage
leading to the quarters of the imperial astrologer.
The moon cast a bright square on the floor,
and the copper buckles of my sandals
glinted
as I trod the patch of brightness.
Hearing footsteps,
I halted.
From the inner chamber,
a slave bearing a torch before them,
three men came forth,
he being one.
He was pale,
but it seemed to me
that the room was lit
not by the torch, but by his countenance.
As he passed, he glanced at me
and said, "I've seen you before, my friend,"
and withdrew to the astrologer's quarters.
Long after his white robes were lost to view
and the torch had been swallowed in darkness,
I stood there, not moving, not breathing,
and afterwards in the barracks,
feeling Martius, who slept next to me,
touch my hand in his usual way,
I pretended to be asleep.
And then one evening
we met again.
We were bathing
near the tents of Caesar's camp,
when suddenly a cry went up.
We ran, but it was too late.
Dragged from the water, the body
lay on the sand,
and that same unearthly face,
the face of a magician,
stared with wide-open eyes.

Still far off, the Emperor was hurrying toward us,
shaken by the grievous tidings;
but I stood seeing nothing,
not feeling tears unknown to me since childhood
running down my cheeks.
All night I whispered prayers,
raving of my native Asia, of Nicomedia,
and angel voices sang:
"Hosannah!
A new god
is given unto men!"

VI. Canopic Ditties

1.

Life's light and free in Cánopus:
there let us sail, sweet friend.
The lightest skiff shall carry us
and speed our journey's end.
See how the inns stand beaconing
along the tranquil crest—
cool terraces are beckoning
the traveler to rest.
We'll take a room together there,
as quiet as we can find,
weave garlands for each other's hair,
sit hour-long hand in hand.
To trade sweet-subtle kisses—
we're no dullards in that school.
The sacred town shall bless us
and make us clean and whole.

2.

Am I not like an apple tree,
an apple tree in bloom?
Say, sweet sisters!
Are not my curls
like its leafy crest?
Is not my body as graceful
as its slender bole?
My arms are as supple as branches,
my legs firm to the earth as roots.

Are not my kisses sweeter than sweet apples?
But ah!
But ah!
The young men stand around in a ring,
eating the apple tree's fruit;
but my fruit,
but my fruit
only one may eat!

3.

Oh we've such a lot of work to do,
we'd best get down to it, and soon:
there's the grapevine's thirsty roots to wet,
the apple's withered twigs to prune.
We've lovely blooms and luscious grapes
in our secluded little plot;
come see—the purple-clustered vine
would gladden anybody's heart.
Charged by Zeus—Celestial Host—
to be unlatched and open wide,
our shrubbery-shrouded wicker gate
beckons to him who passes by.
We'll welcome everyone to our plot
who happens by our wicker gate.
No misers we: come one, come all
and share with us the purple grape.

4.

The Cyprian ranges in pursuit
of Adonis, her beloved youth—
a lioness.
Restless, the goddess roams the strand,
weary, she falls upon the sand,
by sleep unblessed.
Adonis, spectral-white, appears,
his radiant gaze grown dark and blear—
light banished.
Scarce breathing, up she springs once more,
the weariness she felt before
quite vanished.
Swift as the wind the goddess flies
to the shore where fair Adonis lies

lifeless and cold.
Piteously Cytherea moans,
dolefully the sea-wave groans,
sharing her woe.

5.

Whirl faster, step lightly,
join hands, clasp them tightly
like this.
The hiss
of the silvery sistrum is borne, is borne
through the echoing groves, now faint and forlorn.
Can the Nile fisherman know
what the sea will provide
when he casts his nets wide?
Knows the huntsman
when he draws his bow
who shall slay the flying doe?
Knows the husbandman
what his care will avail
his tender vines in the beating hail?
What do we know?
What can we know?
What's to regret?
Whirl faster, step lightly,
join hands, clasp them tightly
like this.
The hiss
of the silvery sistrum is borne, is borne
through the echoing groves, now faint and forlorn.
We know
that all is unsure,
that naught can endure.
We know
that change alone
is to change unknown.
We know that the body we cherish
must utterly perish.
Such is our knowledge,
such our love—
then let us the more tightly cling
to every fleeting, fragile thing.

Whirl faster, step lightly
join hands, clasp them tightly
like this.
The hiss
of the silvery sistrum is borne, is borne
thorough the echoing groves, now faint and forlorn.

VII. Conclusion

Alas, I am forsaking Alexandria
and long shall I not see her.
I shall see Cyprus, dear to the goddess,
I shall see Tyre, Ephesus and Smyrna,
I shall see Athens, the dream of my youth,
Corinth and far Byzantium
and the crown of all longings,
the goal of all strivings—
I shall see Rome the mighty!
All things I shall see, save thee alone!
Alas, my joy, I must forsake thee,
and long, long shall I not see thee!
Many wonders shall I see,
into many eyes shall I gaze my fill,
many lips shall I kiss,
many a curly head caress,
many the names I shall whisper
at the trysting hour in many a grove.
All things shall I see, save thee alone!

1905–1908

*   *   *

Quietly I take my leave of you,
And you stay on the balcony.
"How glorious is our God in Zion"
They trumpet from the Tauride Gardens.
A pale star do I see
In a warm and lucid sky—
No better words shall I find
In taking leave of you:
"How glorious is our God in Zion."

May-October, 1912

Chodowiecki

It may well be that tender Chodowiecki
Was the engraver of my daydreams:
This half-Teutonic garden,
This village house fit for a doll,
These barberry bushes candy-like.

There's been a shower; aery are thoughts.
From windows—orderly clatter of piano scales.
The soul aspires (afar? aloft?),
Raindrops suspended from leaves,
Din of birds along the cornice.

Thunder quiets down beyond the hills,
In a grove a horn responds,
And uncle in round spectacles
Leans over flowers impatiently,
His *Schlafrock* bright with ornamental blooms.

Rainbow and bridge and rider—
I see them all in endless dreams:
Front garden glistening wet,
A groom in a meadow restrains
A stallion straying from the herd.

Who's arriving? Who will take his leave?
But a boy has come out on the porch,
He's sure to forget about his supper,
And a warm wind will long
Caress his open face.

1916

Fuji in a Saucer

Through steaming tea I glimpse Mount Fuji
Against yellow sky and golden volcano.
How oddly a saucer narrows nature—
But a new tremor sends tiny ripples.
Gossamer of fine-stretched clouds
Pierced by an ant-eye sun,
Black tea leaves—are they birds or fish?—
Mask azure of trembling topaz.
The saucer's world will hold a vernal world:
Almonds will be fragrant, horn will blow,
And all the cove—were it twice as broad—
Would be encompassed by the porcelain rim.
And yet a branch of unforeseen mimosa,
Cleaving the heavens, falls across it all—
So in pages of philosophic prose
Sometimes will gleam a line of lovesick verse.

1917

White Night

Luminary over the horizon,
Sonorous absence of sound,
With mirrored green
Have pierced a glassy premonition.
Drowses the slow-paced will,
And seconds are tapped out for eternity:
Expanse of heavenly saffron,
Subterranean resounding dome.
It watches, eye unseeing,
In the still, transparent haze.
And only beyond the heavens, aloft,
Trembles the breath of ethereal life.

1917

Sophia

Gnostic Poems
(1917–1918)

Sophia

In a frail and gilded boat
Through a ranging green,
Through an azure emerald
I awaited longed-for wanderings.
My saffron-scarlet sail
I set to catch the wind,
Vernal fluff of downy osier
I fastened to the stern.
Rapturous and radiant
The molten expanse.
Sisters and brothers go in pairs,
But I am alone in a weightless boat.
On the seven-columned throne
Sapphire-like I blazed,
With undesiring desire
I longed for Thee, O Christ!
I said: "It is unlawful
To shackle the soul with law,
Voluntarily or involuntarily,
I will break the ban on love!"
My chains of hammered gold,
Cloven, have fallen from me ...
Hast Thou forgotten, Father,
Thy beloved daughter?
Sun flies up like a ball ...
My beating heart grows cold ...
Lower, lower ... mountains come in sight ...
Heavier I grow, and heavier ...
I shall spring up like grass,
Like mountain water shall I sing,
And my unfading body
With black soil I shall darken.

Behold, bridegroom, I breathe and I remember
The blessèd habitations—
I am a crucified betrothed,
Sophia is my name!

Basilides

More gigantic than elephants even horses now appear!
Assyrian shabracks press against
The sunken gorges of their foaming flanks,
Fearsome the grin of their bared teeth!
The roistering of the Libyan soldiers,
Who with trumpet and throat glorify their leader,
Is as hard for me to bear
As a burden of crushed cliffs.
I know that there was Homer,
Helen there was, and fallen Troy.
Heroes
Glutted themselves and brawled,
And gods slid down a rainbow . . .
Muse, colossal Muse
Strode flatfooted,
Speaking at the top of her lungs . . .
Sweet Muse, little Muse
With tiny finger has erased
Beginnings that precede the flood.
Now, Sun, don't you go burning—
That's terribly uncouth;
"Give us some dawn, just a little dawn—
Whisper dry lips—
A narrow strip of autumn dawn!"

Today's a strange day.
Superstition, of course, is alien to me,
But this lilac shadow,
These locked doors!
Where to escape this burning heat?
I would drown myself . . .
(Antinous' death!)
But the Nile is dreadfully far.
What if I dig a little pond
Right here in the garden?
It won't be very deep—
That's where I'll go.
If only I had a wall to shelter me!

Life is like nostrils' puff of smoke,
A little pigeon,
Glimpsed far off.
Surely they won't say: "He's dead"?
Never thought
I'd be exchanging a smile for laughter and for tears.
I can't even stand kids
Throwing their ball too noisily.
I made no struggle,
I was weak, my hands hung limp.
Like an unlettered slave
I listened to a slew of pompous interjections.
And all at once
Despite will, despite desire,
Arose a radiant row
Of buildings unimaginable,
From livid space sprang forth a flame.
Herald became a bearded vagabond,
And knowledge loftier than knowledge,
A love more pure than love,
A strength more powerful than strength,
Rapture—
Sphere-like,
Round, uprearing.
Clamorous, seething,
They suffused me with their sorcery.

    Aeon, Aeon, Pleroma,
    Pleroma—Plenitude.
    To the fiery home,
    The enthroning throne,
    To the thunder's ring,
    Spirit of spirits, soar!
Power! Power! Power!
Scourges of flexed muscles!
Shout louder, you children,
Throwing your red ball!
I have learned laughter and tears!
What does Homer mean to me?
A greater force than horses, soldiers, sun, death and the
    Nile—

The crystal harmony
Of the seven-heavened spheres has deafened me.

Tympanum, murmur!
Trumpet, blow!
Howl, strike the ear!
Whirl of pigeons!
Scream of eagles!
Moan of swans!
Hover spirit,
Waft, waft,
Portals
Of paradisal paradise!
Paradise, paradise!
In my hand was a polished stone,
Out of it streamed a bloody flame,
And the word was rudely scraped: "Αβραξαζ."

Faustina

Fish flicks silvery tail,
Star burns yellow in vacant sky—
O Faustina!

Ever closer, lighthouse dark and proud,
Ever quieter, water's splash on broadside—
Stretches the mire . . .

Stray moth has alighted on rudder . . .
How distant the day of our tryst!
Shadow of the Palatine.

Wind has brought mignonette's fragrance.
Rosy spray besprinkles my oar.
O Faustina!

Mentor

Can mentors be roaming arenas?
Don't they live in undisturbed abodes?
(Chiton of azure, of azure!)
Do you wish to resurrect me, do you wish to
Kill me, lips that have robbed me of quiet?
(And whence he comes no one knows.)

Have few or have many days passed
Since last his fingers touched my hand?
(Chiton of azure, of azure!)
Since when have sages dressed their hair like dandies?
Can that yellow gleam before me be a road?
(And whence he comes no one knows.)

I'd liken his polished nails to onyx—
That collar, ah, is sewn with pearls . . .
(Chiton of azure, of azure!)
From wall to wall, the entire circus
Has shuddered to behold a new Adonis.
(And whence he comes no one knows.)

A murmur has come from Bithynia,
Angelic kisses have rustled.
Is the vernal solstice here so soon?

Paces

Your paces in the secluded garden
And voice of turtledove beyond the mountain: "I will come!"
Straight beds of hyacinth are sweet—
But new swarm already seeks new queen,
And the shepherd cuts a fresh pipe.

Spirit twists in prophetic trance;
Like censers of sacrosanct fever
They rustle, skirmishing, the aery whirls of
—Your paces.

In this wearisome hell I'm certain:
On the threshold I'll be finding desert dust!
Porphyrian floors are mirror-smooth . . .
They carry rainbows, resolutions
To the translucent ripened fruit
—Your paces.

Martyr

Twilight, equivocal hour . . .
Ambiguous are all words,
Circles float on the water—
Isn't this a sacred story?
Why this burning in my head,
This sense of trouble brewing?
Barbarian and tender name,
With bread and honey fragrant—
The like of which I've never heard.
In mighty Rome,
Beneath the apostolic sky,
A saint such as this they have never beheld.

Fish

Touching to sit
At the teacher's hand.
The Jewish fishermen
On a flat lake are casting their nets.
Clouds creep snowily—
—Hey there! Got the bread?—
Andrew leaned
Over his patched net.
We are reading in a closed room,
The heart is expecting miracles.
Remember, my son, remember
The brushwood on the barren soil.
Golden banners are suspended
(In the heart, in the water, in the reeds?)
The darker and denser to reason,
The simpler to weightless spirit.
Why so windy in the house?
Why so salty the aromas?
Why so sickly-sweet an odor,
As if it were the hour of death?
Clouds creep snowily . . .
Cast your eyes above the banner—
A naked, doe-eyed Youth.
Leans forward, lifts himself, starts running—
The curve of adolescent thigh.
Next to him a white-hot sun—
Ringing pail with golden depths.
Catch it, catch it! Joyous tidings
Of the mutest of all fish.
I'll throw myself into your nets,
Spindling to the water with a splash!
A white and snowy radiance
Solemn and jesting fans the air.
Brother, beloved, and nurse are you to me,
O Child Divine!
From the eyes scales fall—
Brush them away.
Can it be so childishly easy

To save your soul?
The very same ancestral hall
—Am I asleep, am I dreaming?—
On my hair from the sky have fallen
A fish's golden scales.

Hermes

A guide of spirits, Hermes,
You no longer seem to me.
We have taken our leave of a marshy hell
And you have become a stripling dear to me.
Let us sit down
Above the yellow Nile of evening.
Through an acacia net
Dives the two-horned moon.
Your cheeks are touched with tender down—
There's no caressing them enough!
"Unto the pure—all things are pure,"
Said the Apostle, do you remember?
It grows ever darker in the water meadows—
A cherry your mouth, a sparrow I.
   Is there no echo in your lips
   To my every kiss?
   The boats are all departed,
   Dear one, don't be sad.
   The boats are all departed,
   To distances far-off!
   Don't let clothes get in our way.
   Sting me, sting me, sting!
But what can this indigo light be?
What this mark upon your brow?
Swift wings spring open on your feet.
Where are you? Are you here? You're not?
Horror
Has knotted me tight,
Weakness has overcome me ...
Again I am drowsing in my grave ...
Again the pale pool
(Lead me away, lead me away, O my guide!)
The forest is sickly and languid ...
(The wind drives homeward all the boats)
Hermes, Hermes, Hermes!

Thrall

1. Angel of the Annunciation

Before—
A sweet languor,
Fever of pounding drums—
Dilated pupil,
Breath of airplane tired of flying,
When whirling folds
Of rainbow apparel
Gyred before astounded eye
(The white-robed ones at Jesus' sepulcher
Spake: "Whom seek ye?"
And bearers of myrrh in joyous fear
No longer stand as paupers).
And in a wind with rose's fire
Wings of a flying victory,
Barely
More visible than blood in a tender body.
Curve cast by the boyish flank
Of a Ganymede unknown
And by an eagle—
By plunderer and plundered together
(Milky warmth flows through the mute bride's veins),
And no voice—
But ether of finest gold-dust,
Equal to forces that breach a wall,
Will quiver in the heart: Forward!
"Behold the world!
The turn
Draws near
Of fancy's flying ships
To take from anchor
To the air.
Ploughman's
Sowing,
Having flown up,
Rain-like falls
On otherworldly fields."

Ezekiel's wheel—
His face!
Ezekiel's wheel—
Annunciation!
Turning, it joins all things together,
Bringing all faces to mind,
Although one face alone is visible,
Always the same one.
Here are the beloved, kindred features
That are yours,
Quick gaze of a lady on her way to Tsarskoye,
Countenance of Antinous,
And another,
Glancing, perhaps, from a Hermitage frame,
Wherein sleeps
Rustle of mystery,
Wherein still lives delight
Of mystical, beloved art . . .
Turns, like glistening rose of Adonis' flank,
The lofty messenger of fate,
With messenger of feeling merged—
Gabriel.
   Golden and aery
   Are your trysts, your inspirations.
   But diligent days will bring
   The annunciating vision.
With joyous hand the veil
Is drawn from your spirit,
Psyche—a weightless moth—
Hearkens to ringing quiet.
   O God, two lives are but little
   All to fulfill—
   Two lives, three lives, four.
   So great a field to plough,
   So mighty a harvest to reap.
   But joyous this is, not fearsome . . .
   Only to make a beginning,
   If God would only spare us!
Slap!
They've thwacked our mugs with a filthy rag,
Taken from us bread, light, warmth, meat,
Milk, soap, paper, books,
Clothing, boots, blankets, butter,

Kerosene, candles, salt, sugar,
Tobacco, matches, porridge—
Everything.
And they said:
"Live and be free!"
    Slap!
They've locked us in cages, in barracks,
In an almshouse, in a lunatic asylum,
Having first sown despair and hate . . .
Your ideal—has it not been accomplished, Arakcheyev?
"Live and be free!"
    Slap!
With a slab the breast is burdened,
The very air is different
From what it was
When life was good . . .
Vomit-wearied is the world,
Hangover dregs in the mouth, in the head.
Wan are lantern flares,
From sky and earth—dirt,
Filth,
Slush,
You feel like beating someone up, weeping—
Of such sway can you then dream,
But can it be possible
On a tolerable day,
With a glimmer of sun,
With faint sea breezes
Fetching spring?
Downtrodden
Not even by boots,
Or bast-wrapped feet,
But by shoes stolen from others;
We live in freedom,
Shivering round an unheated stove
(There's inspiration for you!).
In darkness we make our way to friends shivering like us.
Few enough of them there are—
We eat leftovers, greedily eyeing other people's grub.
Too dull the mind
To register attacks.
There aren't any battles, conflagrations.
Cowardly shootings,

Hatred grey,
Dreadful underground existence
Of worms unborn.
Dung
Can we really be?—
That's what the dung heap we're under
(So what if it's breathless and frozen stiff),
Has dubbed us.
  No.
Crushed, terrified,
Abject, perplexed, perhaps—
But we are human beings,
And that's why this is nothing but a dream
(God, a dream that's lasted two whole years)
And it cannot be that for eternity
The angel of annunciation
Has forsaken me.
I'm waiting for him,
With miracle in mind.
I am a man,
And in every sun—
Sun of Russia's Easter Fast,
Mantling with March rose
Cupolas and merchant houses;
Embroidered sun of Italy,
Dividing, like Cellini,
Branch from branch,
Vein from vein;
Sun of Paris, grubby, wet with tears;
Vanilla sun of Alexandria,
Mid lilac mists,
And mirage sands—
The beaming lighthouse of antique days;
In the windswept, windswept
Sun of New York,
That glances at buildings,
At workingmen,
In the way their young millionairess boss does;
In the wintry sun of Onegin,
That glinted slantingly
On "Albert's" windowpanes.
And the sharp sting
Of wine and love

Refracted in a sunbeam
(You remember?);
And in that unheard-of sun,
Probably made in Chicago,
That strays across your pages
In ladies' high heels,
Now across Lithuanian fields,
Now through American streets,
Now through dubious, morning-after rooms,
Now through Chinese eyes of grey;
Capricious, of this world,
Sly one, sometimes upside-down
(That Rhine wine—won't it spill?),
Sun.
I see
That winged gleam
Will come back,
And the voice, and the tremor—
Again three lives will not suffice,
And the heart will sink in sweet despair,
But the angel insists: "It's time.
Brief is your allotted term.
Make haste, make haste!
Is it not joyous, the scratching of pen
In dawn quiet,
Like the pricking of wine's needles?"
    And dream will pass,
    And the world will pass,
    Cross yourself and dry your eyes.
    How pure the air,
    How green the leaf,
    Although there has been no thunderstorm.
Anew the sky is azure-sheened,
Anew cocks crow,
Anew Rhine wine can be uncorked
And perfume won't cost three hundred rubles.
And you don't know what to do:
Write,
Go for a stroll,
Love,
Buy,
Drink,
Simply gaze,

Draw breath,
And live, live!
  And then freely, utterly unburdened,
  Sweetly we'll tie up a bundle
  And freely (you understand? *Freely*) we'll go
  To the hot—maintained by a private individual,
  A free man,
  Who makes two hundred thousand a year
  (then that'll be a huge sum)—
  Baths.
I'm finishing my poem
With a rather nasty word,
Having exposed myself to so many attacks
For that word.
I dare not contradict,
Perhaps I'm making a blunder,
But it was a long while back,
Since then I've changed.
Any unprejudiced reader will be convinced of that.
And there's an English motto
(written in French),
That can be seen
On any cigarette-case, on any bar of soap, on any garter:
"Honi soit qui mal y pense."

2. To Eyes that Meet

Soar, wide wind,
Nets of tall spars,
Horizons of green seas,
Melting dawn ambers—
Rich in all things
These greyish eyes,
Peering sharpsightedly,
Glued, among the posters, to a wall:
Secrets of New York
Along with *Mamzelle Zaza.*
Tristan's Scottish cabin-boy
Chromatically weeps,
Roadstead, roadstead early
Adorned with boats of many colors!
Remember, May was frantic,
Balconies, well-nigh Crimean in their crudity,

Loaded with ladies;
Dark juice of sweet cherries
Tinctured your lips,
And then it came to me: somebody, somebody
In this town is going to be hanged.
Same kind of weather now,
And you get younger and more lovely,
But where is it now, our longing?
If only there were a steamship's whistle,
If only there were a breath of wind,
To ripple the paddle past the pines.
Tighter, ever tighter
Grey knot is pulled about me . . .
Can this be just a fluke,
No more than a poster's deception?
Can you be remote forever
O golden, bygone liberty?
Has the anchor been sucked down by sand,
And we'll sit eternally in an empty Petrograd,
To read each day a new decree,
To wait as old maids do
(O wretched prisoners!),
For the White Guards or the Allies to come,
Or the Siberian admiral Kolchak.
Can that be how it is?
Happy days, where are you now?
The life we loved, where are you?
Soar, wide wind!
Just once, just for a moment,
Like the passing glance
Of eyes with a marine and whitish gleam!

3. Floods

Lifting from the depths all rotten filth,
Raging as if reluctantly,
Tempestuous as if by rote,
Rush shushing, sallow
In black and vacuous whirl—
Floods that got on everybody's nerves.
  Abrupt vortexes greasily spit out
  Now carrion, now cow horn,
  Swollen corner of an icon shelf.

A native with a slow boat hook
Pushes his ferry shallows-ward,
More mute than any scarecrow.
Awaken, swimmer, take comfort, take a glance:
Not all in water and in sky is trash,
Not all the dregs of devastation.
Just like a reader robbed of skill,
Sit at the beginner's desk at school,
And puzzle out forgotten prayers.
A broken thing, no more than that,
Will bring a host of themes to mind
From indestructible dear life.
The downfall that you wildly hymned
Will horrify you and appall—
Commencement of a senseless wake.
And dimly, greedily, deaf and blind,
You'll smell the scent of warm white bread,
The village road, scattered spruce,
And you'll recall the weightless sledge,
And how it is that any man
Is purified on Monday Pure.

4. Lullaby

A warm day will come,
Let us greet it like a gift.
Not a mention of rationing,
Or of those naval barracks.
It's all a dream, just a dream.
You will finish your *Mist behind Bars*—
We'll open up the balcony again
And it'll be fun to read a bit.
Once more we'll be aflame
With a light, enthralling heat,
Setting out on a stroll again
To our friends the antiquarians.
The Rhine wine will glow gaily amber,
Steam curl over the risotto.
"Schlafe, mein Prinzchen, schlaf ein!"—
To quote the words of Mozart's song.

1919

*   *   *

O otherworldly
Evenings!
Time
Of golden-vernal dawns!
In this pathless wild
God's stars
Console, ah, more
Than yesterday.

All things end,
Give it no heed!
Creeping murk now
Comes sleepily.
Mutter of argument . . .
Soon, soon it'll be—
Your breast will be adorned
With a rose.

Pain sweetly implores
Entry to the heart—
Permit us
To fling ourselves skywards!
Striding through gorges,
Light of step,
Comes the blessed bearer
Of God's holy will.

The Lord's choir
Will make the beast tremble.
All is revealed—
Have faith, my friend.
We learned in a moment
(Was it you, was it I?)
That the door to happiness
Had not been closed.

1919

* * *

December frosts the rosy sky,
Black the rooms of this unheated house;
And we, like Menshikov in Beryozov,
We read the Bible and we wait.

We wait. And do we know what for?
Can it be for a redeeming hand?
Cracked are our swollen fingers,
Our shoes have rotted on our feet.

There is no talk of Wrangel now,
Day follows hard on numskull day.
On the golden archangel alone
The sunbeams drowse delectably.

Grant us long-suffering endurance,
A heart that's light, sleep that's sound,
The blest perusal of beloved books,
And a horizon still unchanging.

But should an angel mournfully lean down
And sob: "So shall it always be,"
Then may my guiding star
Fall low, like one outside the law.

No, we are only exiles,
Only exiles, my poor love.
The tender, unimpassioned glow
Of kindred blood shall keep us warm,

Tinting the lips a rosy red—
Not chill this momentary abode.
And we, like Menshikov in Beryozov,
We read the Bible and we wait.

1920

*   *   *

Lost enchantment
Merry winds cannot return!
But the Admiralty is keen
To pierce the cerulean lees.
Broad corridor of the Neva's vista
Summons still, deceitfully;
Prospect of past happiness,
How cruelly false it seems.
I know that all will be as it was
In days of old, as it was last year;
Who has just turned seventeen,
Will have his eighteenth birthday soon.
Summer will come, and stifling heat,
It'll go flying, the child's *cerceau*,
But the wheel of inert nature
Is mechanical and soulless.
Go chasing after willow down,
Stare at river's stillness all day long,
But with a free and loving spirit
You will not bring your dreams to life.
All schemes are niggardly and scant.
Shall we liberate ourselves from fetters?
Or, like relics, ossify,
To the surprise of centuries to come?
And, like tidings of a miracle,
They will unearth our undecaying life,
And say: "What strange lives those people lived:
They could love, they could dream, they could sing!"

May 1921

*   *   *

Not bitter to me are need and thrall—
Neither are hunger or destruction,
But a chill pierces my spirit,
In a moldy trickle swirls decay.
"Bread," "water," "firewood": those words
We've understood and seem to know,
But with every passing hour forget
Other, better words.
Like pitiful excrement we lie
In a trampled, barren field,
And there we'll lie until the hour
The Lord breathe into us a soul.

May 1921

*   *   *

To fling into space
Correspondences oblique
Of mirrored spheres—
Insane parabolas
Ringing, arise
In sprouting stems.

With zodiacal flame
Fields are ablaze,
Ether boils,
But all interstices
Outline a scheme
Of the immobile letters

Of your name!

*   *   *

As girls dream of their fiancés,
We talk of art, the two of us.
O you mystic flock of storks!
Ordered pause in living flights!

Catherine is betrothed to Christ,
In two hearts beats a single soul.
Fickle glow will flee the cheeks,
Eyes light up to their very depths.

Winged, uneven murmuring,
"I love you" almost unpronounced.
With what enraptured lovers' tryst
Shall I compare such evenings!

1921

*   *   *

for Olga Glebova-Sudeikina

"And this is one for hooligans"—said
My charming lady-friend, endeavoring
To put into her weakened voice
All the wild romance of midnight streams,
All the daredevilry, the love, the hopelessness,
All the tipsy bitterness of tragic trysts.
Here heeded, eyes downcast, the distant screech
A novelist, a poet, a composer,
While a gauze night drowsed in the windowpane,
And quiet it was as in a monastery.
            "In a rowboat we were gliding . . .
                Remember how it was!
        We weren't rowing, we were kissing . . .
                Could you have forgotten?"

Three days I was beside myself,
Loving, longing, weeping,
And only the fourth day delivered
My familiar languor,
Foretaste of other lassitudes,
The indrawn breath of other heights.
I thought: "An impassioned line
Having pierced me, must pierce others,
And piercing others will redeem me,
Exchanging calm for longing."

And I made up my mind—
From somewhere came a prompting—
To get an old geography of Russia,
And to number one by one
(Such cataloguing hypnotizes
And carries fancy off into the infinite)
All the provinces, all the cities,
The villages and hamlets,
Such as they have been preserved
In Russian memory.

Kostroma, Yaroslavl,
Nizhny Novgorod, Kazan,
Vladimir, Moscow,
Smolensk, Pskov.

Suddenly a halt,
A doomed pose in provincial style,
With cap pulled down at rakish angle.
    "Remember how it was!"
Everyone will remember, even those
Who have nothing to remember, beginning
An involuntary sigh: no living memory they have.

As the second wave
I wanted to enumerate
Righteous men
And local hallowed spots,
Much as ancient icons
Picture them,
In rows of two or three or four.

Hands folded in prayer,
Eyes lifted heavenwards—
Sounds of Kitezh
In a wintry dawn.

Pechora, Kremlin, forests and Solovki
And Karelian Konevetz, deep-blue Sarov,
Thrushes, foxes, striplings, princes,
And a tribe of Russian holy fools,
And a village circle of pious rites.
    When this tide
    Weakens,
    A new one, a forbidden one,
    Flows inexhaustibly,
    Without processions of the cross,
    Without bells,
    Without patriarchs . . .

Smolder suicidal fires; through pathless tundra
Police won't make it to the Vyg.
Podpolniks, Khlysts and Beguns
And on far-floating islands living graves—

An army outcast and most holy
Of the Free and Sacred Spirit!

   This swarm too has dimmed,
   This too has vanished,
   But the ninth wave
   Is distant yet.
   How fearful it will be,
   O how mighty!
   Amid barren fields
   Gushes a new spring!

Another halt,
Alluringly
With all the fascination
Of departed happiness,
Seemingly irrecoverable,
At once particular and common,
Of the spirit, and of this world,
Ineradicably hopeful
Recoverable—
         "Could you have forgotten?"

Lord above, can it be possible?
Heart, mind,
Arms, legs,
Lips, eyes,
Entire being
Will cry out:
"If I forget Thee?"

Next
(A bold and unexpected move)
Out of the blue
Some pages from "All Petersburg"
For 1913, say—
Business firms,
Especially wholesalers:
Leather goods, saddles,
Fish, sausages,
Textiles, papermakers,
Confectioners, bakeries—
A kind of biblical abundance—

Where did it go?
The flour exchange,
Lard, timber, blubber . . .
There's more to offer, more . . .
Fairs . . . there they are
In Nizhny, contracts, and yet more . . .
Shipping companies . . . The Volga!
The Volga, just imagine!
There's more there than just
Stenka's rock (believe me).
And after tormenting myself to the limit
With things most everyday and dear
Let me end on a sudden lyrical note
With snatches from the Russian daily round
And Russian nature:
Apple orchards, fur coats, meadows,
Bee gardens, wide grey eyes,
Thaw, sledges, paternal home,
Birch groves, fresh-mown fields on every side.

  That way it'll be fine.

Like threading beads on a string
Piercing the hearts of listeners.
But everything turned out quite differently—
And I fell into the trap myself.
My own imaginings and words
Turned out to be a novel poison.
I began remembering, for instance,
That springtimes came, "Albert's" existed,
That life once bore some resemblance to life,
That you and I were younger then,
But now all dreams are without a goal,
But a song has a life of its own,
And, you know, a poet's not much good
If he can't keep his own lines in order.

1922

*   *   *

No governor's lady with officer conversing,
No empress lending her ear to an orderly,
On a gilded, twisting stool
At her sewing sat the Mother of God.
And before her stood Archangel Michael
Spur resonant on golden spur,
His stallion tapping hoof at palisade,
While on hillock linen was stretched white.
Said Queen of Heaven to Archangel:
"I just don't know, dear Michael,
What to think. No comfort to the ear.
Devoid of name a country cannot be.
There is no salvation in initials alone.
There is no living without faith and hope,
And without a tsar sent down by God above.
I am a woman. I feel sorry even for a villain.
But these I don't consider human.
Their very selves they have rejected,
Renouncing their immortal souls.
To you I hand them over. Be just."

She fell silent, never putting by her sewing.
No tears glinted on her lashes;
And frowning stood Archangel Michael,
Sun glowing fiery on his armor.
"Well, God be with you," said the Mother of God,
Then quietly glanced out of the window,
And added: "Another week will pass
And the linen will be whiter than snow."

1924

Fourteenth of December

In this fearsome city of shades,
of dreams, of longings unfulfilled,
of winds, of ice,
life flowed on unchanging,
as always.
Eternally youthful, the capital
makes merry, just as in a fairytale;
glitter of balls
and, rare nightmare apparition—
Pugachov.
Sudden, ominous tocsin's toll,
and reverberation shook
Peter's city,
thunder of cannon fire
all night long.
Above us hovers the soul of Sand—
Better death than life as slaves,
Brothers, into battle!
Liberty's flaming banner
High we'll raise!
Faces turn deathly in the murk,
the heart's a captive bird.
Dream or delirium?
O with the tyrant to do battle!
Strength have we none.
As if our wings were clipped,
as if we were and were not,
again it's suffocating.
All our daydreams have drifted away—
blood alone . . .
Could it be that in an instant
all that's sacred, undecaying
in the foam and murk of this black night
has been carried away?
Peace to those who won't return,
who at the hour of reckoning gave

of their blood
and fell in battle
on the Senate Square.

1920s

The Trout Breaks the Ice

for Anna Radlova

First Prologue

The stream is hankering after ice:
Taught by the wintry sky.
Its chains of sugar candy
Twang brittlely as lute strings.
Thrust, trout, with a will!
The sun's aquamarine,
The fleeting bird-shadows—
Are you not weary of them?
The fiercer your convulsions,
The harsher their echo; friendship's return.
On the ice a peasant stands.
The trout breaks the ice.

Second Prologue

When visitors come knocking
And stay unasked to tea,
A man must make them welcome
Or fail in courtesy.

Their eyes are lamps extinguished,
Their waxen fingers gleam,
Beggared the light that glosses
Each threadbare trouser seam.

Titles from oblivion,
Words that never were . . .
A riddling kind of chatter
That leaves the mind a blur . . .

Stamps a capricious heel
The painter long sea-slain,
Next a hussar, a stripling,
With a bullet through his brain . . .

And you're not even born yet,
Dear Mister Dorian—
What business have you lounging
So coolly on my divan?

Well, memory's a hoarder,
Fancy an errand boy—
This prank will cost you dearly
If ever I have my way!

Thrust the First

Winter in the streets, and at the opera—"Tristan."
The wounded sea sang in the orchestra,
The land of green beyond the azure haze,
The heart brought to a shuddering standstill.
Who saw her enter? No one. She was simply
There in serene possession of her box,
A beauty from a painting by Bryullov.
Such women live in the pages of novels,
On the screen too they are to be encountered . . .
Terrible crimes are committed for their sake,
Their carriages are besieged by loyal admirers,
For love of them poison is swallowed in garrets.
She sat there unselfconsciously absorbed
In the unfolding tale of fatal love,
Leaving unstraightened the scarlet shawl
That had stolen from a pearly shoulder,
Caring not at all that she was the target
Of many an unwavering binocular.
And I, who did not know her, I too peered
(Was she alone?) into that shadowy box.
I'd just come from a spiritualist seance,
Though spirits aren't my line, and the medium,
A seedy Czech, had seemed to me pathetic.
Through the window came a flood of light,
Pallid and chill, and with a bluish tinge,
As if the moon was shining from the north:
Iceland, Greenland, ultimate Thule,
The land of green beyond the azure haze . . .
This I remember: my every nerve was bound
By such a languor as precedes eruption,
Expectation mingled with revulsion,
Ultimate shame, consummate bliss . . .
And something within me knocking, knocking,
(The thrusting tail of a fish immured in ice) . . .
Staggering I rose, blindly, like a sleepwalker,
I reached the door. Suddenly it opened.
From the anteroom emerged a man,
He seemed about twenty, and his eyes were green;

Taking me, perhaps, for someone else,
He shook my hand and said: "Care for a smoke?"
How the fish lashed, with what wild urgency!
Who spurns the will attains a higher will.
Ultimate shame, consummate bliss!
The land of green beyond the azure haze.

Thrust the Second

The horses rear in terror,
Entwined with a band of blue,
Wolves, snow, gunfire, bells a-jingle!
What of the reckoning, black as night?
Will your Carpathians not tremble?
Honey harden in the ancient horn?

The sled-rug flaps, a wonder-bird;
Screech of runners—"Maritza, whoa!"
Halt . . . a footman with a lamp comes running . . .
So that's the lair you've made a home of:
Madonna's radiance at your bed-head,
A horseshoe guards your threshold,

Colonnades, a snowdrift on the roof,
Behind the wainscoting mice scamper,
Shabracks, knotted lace and carpets.
Oppressive are the formal bedrooms.
A whole felled forest fills the hearth,
Resin sputtering like incense . . .

But why then have your lips turned yellow?
Do you not know on what you've ventured?
No laughing matter here, my friend.
No vampire from Bohemian woods
You swore to be—but a brother in blood,
The world's your witness. Be a brother!

The prison laws that govern us,
Ah they are obdurate and strict:
Blood for blood and love for love.
We're honor bound in what we give and take,
Of blood vengeance we have no need:
God alone will free us from our oath,

Cain pronounces judgment on himself . . .
The youthful master has turned pale,

And drawn a knife across his palm . . .
Quietly drips the blood into the glasses:
Sign of exchange and sign of safeguarding . . .
The horses are led out into the stable.

Thrust the Third

Like a wing, a wing shot through,
Hangs the ship: a model sloop.
The radiance of a hothouse
Lurks in the glazing of such libraries.

Yesterday's journey and the knife,
The oaths in frenzy taken
Held seeds of falsity for me,
A parody of fearsome crime . . .

I felt like asking . . . What a shame . . .
But this manly kind of ease
Hinted strongly that this spot
Was not intended for such talk.

You have just gone out, Shakespeare
Lies open, cigarette smoke drifts . . .
"The Sonnets"! How simple the world is
To the March lilt of a question.

As embroidery of snowflakes
Melts at vernal ray's assault,
In such a way a young man's life
May follow a capricious path.

Thrust the Fourth

This breakfast, how it brings to mind
Those orchestrated interludes
When every sound and every thought
Awakes its loving opposite:
The clarinet and horn converse,
The flute sleeps in the harp's embrace,
Bodes the funereal trombone—
A sound appealing to the dead alone.
This breakfast how it brings to mind
A sideshow with its Siamese twins;
A single stomach, but two hearts,
Two heads and yet a single spine ...
How can such freaks of nature be?
The answer is a mystery.
Express our traffic literally—
A freak show for the world to see.

You're awakening—I'm awake,
We are two wings—a single soul,
Two souls we are—our maker one,
Two makers we—a single crown ...
But why the suitcase packed and locked,
The railroad ticket ready booked?
This breakfast, how it brings to mind
Some lie insidious and bland.

Thrust the Fifth

The month of May we pass in country style:
The blinds are down, we go about in shirtsleeves,
We've dragged the billiard table to the hall.
And half the day, from breakfast time to tea,
We push the balls around. An early supper,
Then up at dawn for swimming, indolence.
You having left, it seemed appropriate
To live as parted lovers ought to do:
A life of somewhat humdrum healthiness.
I wasn't much expecting letters,
And started when I saw the postmark "Greenock."
"We're spending May in wild delirium,
The rose runs riot and the sea is blue,
And Eleanor is lovelier than ever!
Forgive me, friend—if only you could see her
Of a morning in the flower garden,
Dressed in her dove-grey riding habit
You'd understand that passion conquers will."
Then that was where it was, the land of green!
Who would have thought that tranquil scenery
Could not be backdrop to catastrophe?

Thrust the Sixth

Red-haired, red-cheeked, the sailor left
To sail the distant main.
The years wear on, the beard grows hoar—
He did not come again.
Year in, year out, his grandam prayed
God grant his spirit rest,
And heavy lay the icy weight
On his betrothed's breast.
The table has been cleared long since,
The house cur gnaws a bone—
It lifts its head and starts to howl . . .
In the doorway stands a man.
A sailor he, of years two score.
—Who's master here? Come say!
I carry tidings from afar
For Mistress Annie Ray.
—What tidings can you have to tell?
My man long dead is he!—
He rolled his sleeve back, and behold
The birthmark plain to see.
—Then welcome me, your Erwin Green!—
The fainting bride sinks down.
The father weeps, the mother too,
And kisses her son's brow.
Merrily ring the bells around,
"Ding-dong" through dell and dene.
To church to wed goes Annie Ray,
And with her Erwin Green.
The skirling bagpipes pipe them home,
They're left alone at last.
Said she: I beg you, husband mine,
To set my mind at rest:
Many a strange land you saw
While I lived lonely here—
Have you forgot the holy law
Of your own land and dear?
You spurn the sacraments, I mark,
Nor do you bend the knee,

Nor with a loud amen assent
When the choir sings joyously,
From the holy font you stay your hand
And sit you down uncrossed—
O do not say your heart has banned
Our Savior Jesus Christ . . .
—Lie calm, lie easy, Annie Ray,
And leave this foolish talk!
You've never seen, 'tis clear as day,
The northernlandish folk.
Green is the light that glimmers there
From earth to heaven's rim,
A flower from the water rises clear—
A heart upon a stem,
And brighter shines the icy star
To hearts that know no fear.
If you would see your plighted lord,
Gaze boldly on me here!—
She lifts her eyes and long she stares,
Her mind reels in amaze.
The mariner of two score years,
The partner of her days,
Stands tall and of a noble frame,
Smooth-skinned as any boy,
Proud temple, brow and silken lash—
She cannot look away!
As fresh as any rose he gleamed,
His cheek was rosy-red,
So fresh, so fair he had not seemed
In boyhood days long fled.
His hair is fine as finest flax,
His lips are burning fire,
His eyes are glittering and green,
Miraculous their power . . .
Then all at once it came to her
How many years ago
The young lord at the break of day
Had given up the ghost.
He lay a lily in the tomb,
His grieving mother by;
"How sweet it were," a soft voice came,
"With such a lad to lie!"
Soft whirring and vibrating blue,

And lights swam all around;
Sunk in a green and icy sleep,
The dreaming house slept sound.
She burns and shakes, her salt tears flow,
To pray she has no might.
He waits upon her "yes" or "no" . . .
Soft whirring fills the night . . .
—Ye may be the devil come from hell
My mortal soul to damn,
But devil or no, I love thee well,
Thy bride till death I am!

Thrust the Seventh

The bathing lad—a stranger—
Is bathing on the sly.
He nervously looks about him
With an uneasy eye.
In vain you seek to cover
Your bashful nakedness—
You present no interest
To the village passers-by.
Crossing yourself, but lightly
You dive down from the steep . . .
But were you a bit cleverer,
You'd be Narcissus' self.
And the dragonflies, the midges,
That scorching village sun . . .
You're gazing straight into the sky,
And from the earth you're far . . .
A hint? A recollection?
Submerged, your body
Gleams, is luminescent
With the green of mica.
Hold your swimming to the left
And you'll swim aground.
Lashing in the water there—
A trout, a silver trout!

Thrust the Eighth

Caught in crystal, the sunbeam decomposes
To its elements—you see the rainbow quicken
And points of light leap blithely round the room.
Unless we die we cannot be reborn.
I stepped outside; roses were darkening,
Smelling of Good Friday in the flower-filled church.
The crimson-flooded sky of sunset
Was swallow-streaked, the pond was all aglow.
Dust billowed from the distant herd. Suddenly
A motorcar comes streaking like an arrow
(A sight that's most uncommon hereabouts)
A cloak of green is streaming in the wind.
Dazed by the swiftness of these happenings,
I was gazing into two green eyes,
Two other hands were warmly grasping mine
And, dusty from the road, the weary face
Aroused familiar love, familiar pain.
—Here I am . . . I have no strength . . . I'm done for.
Our transfiguring angel has abandoned me.
A little and my blindness will be total,
A rose will be a rose, the sky the sky,
And nothing more. Mere dust, I shall return
To dust. My blood and bile and brains and lymph
Are desiccated utterly. My God!
Nothing to draw strength from, no exchange!
Walls of unshatterable glass imprison me,
I'm threshing like a fish!—And your green cloak?—
—What green cloak?—Surely you arrived in one.—
—That was a mirage. There isn't a green cloak.—
American dustcoat, kid gloves, grey tie
And a cape the tender hue of *rose champagne*.
—Stay with me here!—You know that cannot be!
Each passing day I seem to sink in deeper.—
His face became a quivering net of nerves,
As if a vivisector stood beside him.
A kiss, and in a moment he was gone,
His motorcar below had long been puffing.
Five days later I received a letter

Stamped with the same odd postmark: "Greenock."
—I meant to write before, but you agree,
Laxness may be pardoned in a happy man,
And happiness for me is—Eleanor,
As a window is a window or rose a rose.
It's ridiculous, isn't it, after all,
To maintain that behind the form of words
Some kind of "higher meaning" lies concealed.
I'm happy then—just simply, sanely happy.
For a letter to arrive here takes five days.

Thrust the Ninth

I invite not friends, but "people I know":
With them it's easier to pass the time.
Of what is past I feel no need to talk,
And what's the point of trying to tell the future?
Not revelry but orderly enjoyment,
Smooth words, words that are agreeable,
White wine leaves no heavy hangover,
An empty head is lucid, clear.
Every hour is filled so carefully
That a single day could well hold forty,
And the epiderm is gently tickled
By that we give the general name of love.
And to keep a changing round of faces,
Not to attach oneself too much to one.
How could balderdash about a land of green
Have simply come into my head?
—You've passed out?—In a metaphorical sense.
—Greenock?—It exists. A Scottish townlet.
Metaphors cloud the atmosphere like smoke,
But vanish in a ring below the ceiling,
Sober day disperses all chimeras—
Many an example can be cited.
With waters of green the river roars,
We cannot save the small canoe.
In a kid glove, a beckoning hand
Will summon you always from afar,
But Erwin Green the mariner
You shall not clasp yet to your heart.

Thrust the Tenth

Sometimes the round of favorite pleasures
Becomes more tedious than sitting at a desk.
Then chance, and only chance, can rescue us,
But chance is no pet dog to come at beck and call.
The temple of chance is the gaming house.
The fervency of flaming eyes,
Parched lips and brows of deathlike hue
I'll not describe. The croupier's rasped edicts
Became the music of my waking nights.
I felt as if I were sitting under water.
The green baize put in my mind
The land of green beyond the azure haze . . .
But memories I did not seek to waken,
Rather I sought to put them from my mind,
Waiting for chance's nod. One evening
A personage in heavy spectacles
Walked across to me and said:—I see
You're not a gambler, but rather an amateur,
Or, more probably, a seeker after sensation.
Admit, though, it's too dreary here for words:
Monotonous and quite uninteresting.
It's early yet. Perhaps you'd care to see
The small collection of curios that I've
Put together? I've been all over Europe,
Been traveling since I was a boy—seen Egypt too.
Over the years it's grown to quite a museum—
You might find a thing or two to amuse you.
All collectors—and I'm no exception—
Are grateful for an audience; unshared,
This passion, like all others, is a dead thing.—
I consented at once, although to tell
The truth, the man did not appeal to me:
He seemed a bore, and a stupid one at that.
Still, it was only quarter to one,
And I certainly had nothing else to do.
Not much, you'll say, of an adventure!
We walked three blocks; the usual kind of entrance,
The usual middle-class apartment,

The usual collection of scarabs,
Arquebuses, broken telescopes,
Moth-eaten perruques, keyless clockwork dolls.
A languid web seemed wound about my brain,
Nausea came on me, my head began to spin,
And I prepared to make my excuses . . .
My host was at a loss, stammered and said:
—I'm afraid this isn't to your liking.
But of course it won't impress a connoisseur.
I have one final hope of pleasing you,
If you'll forgive its uncompleted state,
As yet I haven't found its other half.
One of these days I hope to bring it off.
Perhaps you'll take a glance? A twin.—A twin?
—A twin.—One of a pair?—One of a pair.—
We went into a tiny room: in the middle
Stood an aquarium; its top was covered
With a sheet of glass, blue-tinged like ice.
A trout made melancholy curves within,
Beating melodiously against the glass.
—That fish will break the glass, be sure of that.
—But where's this twin of yours?—A moment, patience.—
He opened, smirking, a cupboard in the wall,
Skipping back behind the door. On a chair inside,
Against a backcloth of green calico,
Reclined a ragged creature, sunk in sleep
("Caligari!"—a lightning flash of thought):
Green translucence lurked beneath the skin,
The lips' curl told of crime and bitterness.
About the forehead clustered auburn curls
And in the dry temple a vein was throbbing.
With expectation and revulsion
I stared, unable to take away my eyes . . .
Softly the fish was beating at the ice . . .
An aery tinkling mingled with a peal of blue.
The American dustcoat and the neatly knotted tie.
The cap the tender hue of *rose champagne*.
He smote his chest and shouted in a frenzy . . .
—Good God, you mean to say you know each other?
And even . . . perhaps . . . I can't believe my luck!
—Open up your eyes, your eyes of green!
I take you as you are, in whatever guise
The land of green has sent you back to me.

We are blood brothers. In the Carpathians,
You remember, Shakespeare still lies open
And radiant words dissolve in rainbows.
Ultimate shame, consummate bliss.—
The thrusting fish deals blow on blow on blow.

Thrust the Eleventh

—You're breathing? You're alive? You're not a ghost?
—The firstborn I of green vacuity.

—I hear your beating heart, your blood is warm.
—Those whom love has summoned may not die.

—Your cheeks are redder, and corruption fades . . .
—A secret interchange is taking place . . .

—What is it first meets your restored gaze?
—I see a trout, a trout that breaks the ice.

—Lean on my arm. And make an effort. Rise.
—Fabric given airing takes on strength.

—Will you put your green languor out of mind?
—I set my foot upon a higher step.

—And can your spirit once again take fire?
—Copper is welded by fire to gold.

—Has the transfiguring angel come again?
—Yes, the transfiguring angel has come again.

Thrust the Twelfth

On the bridge the horses glisten,
Caparisoned with snow,
And palm to palm tight pressing,
We swiftly gallop home.

There are no words but only smiles,
No moon, but burns a star—
Changes and mistakes
Like water flow away.

Along the Neva, round a canal
And up the carpeted stairs
You hasten as in days of yore,
Into the familiar house.

Two garlands made of porcelain,
Two sets of knives and forks,
And in your steady gaze of green
Two roses upon stalks.

The hallway clock is audible
Slowly beating twelve.
And my trout resoundingly
Breaks the remaining ice.

Are we alive? We're living still.
We're dead? O enviable tomb!
Paying age-old custom honor,
The bottles pop their corks.

No place here for melancholy,
For doubting or for care.
Through the doorway comes the golden-haired,
The lunatic New Year.

Epilogue

You know my original intention
Was to depict the twelve months of the year,
Devising for each of them a proper role
In the carefree round of amorous diversion.
And just look at the result! Clearly
I'm not in love and not so light of heart.
Memories came flooding in upon me,
Snatched from novels read long since;
The dead joined company with the living,
And such a muddle came of it that I
Feel sorry I started the whole business.
The twelve months I've kept at any rate
And indicated, more or less, the weather.
That's something. For the rest, it's my belief
A trout can break the ice that prisons it
If only it persevere. And that is all.

1927

In Memoriam Lydia Ivanova

Behest, recollection or alarm?
Why are the poplars trembling again?
In windlessness a weary sound has faded,
Warmth and life have abandoned the fields.

An enchanted land came in a dream,
Fountains of violins, silver tulle;
That lovely spring did not divine
It was not fated to meet July.

Disappeared. A pause. The sheen is mute.
An echo is sole answer to the question.
And in a faint scent we may hazard
Fragrance of otherworldly roses . . .

April 1927

*   *   *

for Olga Cheremshanova

Were I a painter, I would paint
A maiden sanctuary behind a lofty palisade,
And a peacock ridge slumbers far away
Keeping watch over Siberian reaches.
And seated is a maid of flint—
A black swan turned to stone,
Casting no glance, saying no word, paying no heed;
A new song has locked her lips,
Swirling only from the depths.
Strike, strike at the flint, young master,
Strike at the liver, at the heart,
In an instant sparks, and flame, and madness.
The terrible dove has taken wing,
The mare has forgotten the herds,
Tossing to the wind her mane,
Sapphire gleams the Grecian sea.
Black supplication whirls,
The ancient chant is resurrected,
The blaze has leapt from roof to roof,
What shall we see, good friends, what hear?
Wild ardor of a lithe *gitana*,
Cicada crackle of castanets,
Fringes of eyelash and shawl,
Between the teeth a scarlet rose.

No matter that the skirts are ripped!
A gypsy girl can make do with little.
Cooing of concordant tambourines,
Turtledoves doubling in mountain heights.

You've remembered? O-le!
You've shuddered? O-le!
Memory is like a knife buried deep,
Plunged in smoky muskmelon of days!

And when on some lively dancing-floor
In Berlin, say, or in Vienna,

You enter modestly arrayed,
Carousers and idle loafers
Will set their eyes on a maid of flint,
They'll be confused in their flat-bottomed hearts:
Why is it so foreign, so familiar
This hidden flame,
This will obscure and wild,
These waves of ritual blackness.
Her eyes are as if shuttered with night,
Her lips are hung with a sacred lock.
Touch her—and your body reels,
As though a wet hand grasped a cable.
And the lowering brow gives utterance
To what's most ancient, unexampled, new.

1927

Settlers

An alien sun beyond an alien swamp
Roosts frantically upon its perch.
And tomorrow autocratically will rise anew
Not punishing, not conferring favor.
How coarse, Molly, your hands have grown
And how he's gone to seed, that cheery Dick of yours -
The one who kept you laughing with his boxing tales
When you were sailing on the packet boat.
Into the den, and quick! Malaria's breath
Creeps in with the lilac twilight
Through the ill-caulked walls.
The frugal lamp is smoking,
And Granny's Bible lies wide open.
How scrawny, Molly, your hands have grown;
Your beauty, how it has withered,
And you expecting your fourth child.
The three you have are anemic, undernourished,
Fated to dry out with their bones
This terrain unfit for living.
O God, God, God, God, God!
What's the point of waking up, if tomorrow
You see same road, same mounds,
Stick standing with a sign "Avenue of Victories,"
A wretched stall and a tavern at the crossroads,
Plus fenced-in puddle—that's the Capitol.
And the children will grow up like swineherds:
Forgetting how to read, to write, to pray,
They'll be picking at the mean soil,
And saying over and over—"Time is money."
In the Pantheon they'll swarm pointlessly,
Spitting chewing gum on the marble.
Invent contraptions for cleaning boots,
Multiply and dumbly die
Hardly aware of the boring glory
Of the delusive word: "Pioneers."
Better to sleep till midday, Molly—
Perhaps you'll dream of the bank of the Thames,
And the ivy-covered house where you were born.

1927

Theater

The Death of Nero

A Play in Three Acts and Twenty-Eight Tableaux
Dedicated to Sergei Radlov

ACT I
1st Tableau

Rome. A hotel room. Dusk. PAVEL and MARIE.
MARIE stands by the window. 1919.

PAVEL. Do you have the key to the suitcase?
MARIE. But all the same I hate you!
PAVEL. I wasn't talking about that at all.
MARIE. But all the same I hate you!
PAVEL. Always the tragic buskin!

A silence.

MARIE. How golden the sky is today! I've never seen one like
   it!
PAVEL. But I have! (*MARIE doesn't turn round.*) I have! Long
   ago. About ten years. The whole day I was tramping
   around, trying to find some money. I knew that my mother
   and sister were at home. The three of us hadn't eaten for
   three days. That wasn't hard on me, but on such occasions
   they always remembered they were Christians and heaped
   abuse on me, or they kept silent in such a way that it was
   worse than any abuse. It was the second month I hadn't
   been able to find a job. No one would give me any money.
   I went to see an old school friend. He'd managed to set
   himself up in luxury but kept assuring me that he didn't
   have a penny. He begged me to stay for lunch. I saw a table
   set with a bottle and white bread. I declined the invitation.
   My head was spinning, and I had such a feeling of light-
   ness. I felt as if I could fly, burst into song, write poetry, get
   into conversation with the first lady I met. And it was then
   the sky was so golden. Just once.

131

MARIE. Yes, Pavel, you know how to suffer privation, but I
hate you all the same.

PAVEL. I don't believe you.

MARIE. You may be right. I have moments when someone
speaks inside of me. It isn't me, but some kind of devil. And
everything is extraordinarily clear and disgusting. And I'm
disgusting myself. Then it passes.

PAVEL. Perhaps that is what is real?

MARIE. Enough of this. We have to wash and change for
dinner.

PAVEL. I cannot live without you!

MARIE. I know.

2ⁿᵈ **Tableau**

Rome. A hotel room. A neighboring room separated
by an arch. The table there is laid for supper.
PAVEL is seated at a small table and is finishing
reading aloud from a manuscript. MARIE and some
visitors listen. On a chair by the door sits POMPEO;
his costume is such as to arouse suspicion.

PAVEL (*reading*).—There's loyalty for you!—he dies. A centurion covers the body with a cloak. The sun rises. The end.

Closes his notebook. Everyone is silent.

Well, that's it!

Everyone remains silent.

VOICES (*gradually increasing in strength*). Of course, it's very
original, but as far as truth to history is concerned . . . It
isn't clear where the author's sympathies lie. The commu-
nists will be satisfied. The fascists, too. Aren't you attribut-
ing feelings and concepts of our own to the Romans? The
female types are like caricatures. Not much in the way of
the majestic—after all, it is imperial Rome, and that
should be on a grand scale. Too hysterical. Even we have
grown unaccustomed to decadent anguish. (*A woman's
voice: "I defend the scene with the violets and the little bird."*)
A muddle. Hardly suitable for the stage. Greatly lacking in
respect. A man should have something he holds sacred!

Marie quickly goes over to PAVEL and presses his
hand. He doesn't get up.

MARIE (*without releasing PAVEL's hand*). Ladies and gentlemen, Pavel Andreyevich has written drama, not historical
research. What matters here is imagination and expressiveness. That's why everything seems close to us, modern.
How else is he to write? It may well be that among us, in
this very room, suchlike Neros are to be found—that's what
counts and that's what we feel. But now perhaps you would
like to have a bite to eat. That's where we'll continue our
discussion. Wine loosens the tongue and brings ideas to
mind.

All pass into the next room, except for PAVEL,
MARIE and POMPEO.

PAVEL. Marie!
MARIE. Well, then? Aren't I wonderful, getting everybody
out of a tricky situation?
PAVEL. Can that really be true?
MARIE. Can what be true?
PAVEL. What you were saying.
MARIE. Probably. Why should I have spoken otherwise?
Magnanimity is something I don't suffer from.
PAVEL. Marie!
MARIE. Time to get back to our guests. (*Exit.*)
POMPEO (*goes over to PAVEL and hands him a letter*). Your Ex-
cellency, a letter. I couldn't steal a moment to give it to you,
so I listened to every bit of your fine creation. I applaud
you. Terrific job! If I may be allowed to speak frankly,
though, all this is only a dream! Action is what we need.
Action will save mankind.
PAVEL. Who are you?
POMPEO. Crooked Pompeo.
PAVEL. What's crooked about you?
POMPEO. It's a nickname. I don't know.
PAVEL. I will go where I am summoned.
POMPEO. Of that we had no doubt.
PAVEL. Oh, so you had no doubt?
POMPEO. Don't be suspicious. We know the kind of man you
are and what it is you're looking for—that's enough for us.
MARIE (*appearing in the doorway*). Pavel!

POMPEO bows and goes out.

Who on earth is that?

PAVEL. An acquaintance of mine.

MARIE. I don't care what kind of acquaintances you have, you know that. But you mustn't confuse daydreaming with action. They are two entirely different things. A great misfortune could happen.

PAVEL. To whom? To me?

MARIE. Maybe not only to you.

3rd Tableau

A house in the provinces occupied by LEPIDA.
Winter. A fire in the hearth. LEPIDA and two
maidservants sit at their spinning.

LEPIDA. It's a bit cold, Pudentilla. Did you put enough wood on the fire?

PUDENTILLA. I did. It was you who gave the order to economize. We don't have much firewood left.

They spin.

SIDONIA. Few apples did we gather this year.

LEPIDA. Everything is running at a loss, you might say.

PUDENTILLA. Different from the old days. Remember how many we picked five years back? Two larders packed to the ceiling—you couldn't open the doors, apples would come tumbling out. And lots were piling up outside as well, the serving-folk had the runs for two months.

LEPIDA. Fulvia writes that in Rome there are shortages—of food, of flour, of firewood.

SIDONIA. It's not often she writes to you.

LEPIDA. What do you want? That's the way people are. You prosper and they cling to you, but just let something happen and you won't find anyone with a bloodhound. When it became known that Agrippina was going into exile, it was as if the house had a curse upon it—not a soul to be seen. Aren't many fools like me around.

SIDONIA. But one day she'll be grateful to you.

LEPIDA. Perhaps. Who can tell? She may well take me to court for the inheritance. And she won't give it a thought that providing her son with an upbringing and an education cost me money. I'm not some kind of moneybags either, just a poor widow.

PUDENTILLA. The gods will not abandon you for your kindness.

> NERO, six years old, comes running in, followed by his dancing master and barber.

NERO. Auntie, auntie, just look what I've got to show you!

LEPIDA. Good day, Nero. Well, what are you going to show that I've never seen before?

NERO. No, no need to get up, just sit still. Only move your chair back and watch! I've learned a new dance. What's it called?

DANCING MASTER. The cachucha.

NERO. The cachucha. It's Spanish, you'll see.

> He dances with castanets.

MAIDSERVANT (*while Nero is dancing*). What a sweet little laddie! Just look at him making eyes! And he's so nimble! Though you wouldn't exactly call him slim. O, the shame of it—the way he wiggles his backside! That Pertinax certainly knew what to teach him!

> NERO finishes and flings himself on his aunt's neck.

NERO. Was I good?

LEPIDA. Not bad at all. If you like that sort of thing—not bad.

PUDENTILLA. Very good, little Nero, very good! Just seven years or so and you'll be driving everyone crazy.

NERO. That I don't want. Crazy people scare me; dogs bark at them.

PUDENTILLA. I didn't mean it that way. It's you folk will go crazy about.

LEPIDA. Now that's enough! What kind of idiocy is that! He's only a boy—he doesn't understand.

PUDENTILLA. Come off it! Just show me those boys who don't understand. Last time I gave him a wash ...

LEPIDA. Enough of that! So you washed him and that was that—now you can shut up! This is what you'd better tell me, Nero. Naturally, you'll have read the life-stories of all kinds of heroes, great men, and so forth. Which of them would you choose for yourself as a model?

NERO (*after some thought*). Alcibiades' dog!

LEPIDA. What do you mean, Alcibiades' dog?

NERO. Oh auntie, it was an absolutely marvelous dog! They chopped off its tail, painted it green all over. It was all that people talked about. Ran after it in crowds, they did. A marvel it was!

LEPIDA. What nonsense are you filling the boy's head with, Pertinax? What's the point of that?

PERTINAX. Forgive me, mistress—the dog was mentioned just in passing. No fault of mine it stuck in Nero's head. Besides, that's something I don't specialize in. I warned you that I was just a dancing master.

LEPIDA. A dancing master! But you are literate. I hired you to teach him all subjects. If I could read myself, I wouldn't have given you a thought. In future I intend to be present at his lessons . . . Alcibiades' dog!

NERO. Auntie, are we having breakfast soon?

LEPIDA. No, it'll be some time yet. You want to eat already?

NERO. I do.

LEPIDA. Good. Patience, Nero. We're in trouble—you and your mother, too, the whole family. You mustn't forget you have to endure it so the gods may witness. Then they will take pity on you.

NERO. I don't want anyone to take pity on me!

LEPIDA. So what do you want?

NERO (*irritably*). I want people to love me.

LEPIDA. What a funny child!

The maidservants laugh.

4th Tableau

The hotel. A downstairs vestibule. People arrive
and depart. Sunshine from the street. The vestibule
is cool and somewhat gloomy. A light is burning.
Enter MARIE and PAVEL. MARIE puts an armful of
flowers on a wicker table and sits down in a wicker
armchair without removing hat and gloves.

PAVEL. Tired?

MARIE. Why should I be? Didn't we come here by car?

PAVEL. I don't know. The air, it could be.

MARIE. There are too many flowers here. It's irritating.

PAVEL. But you love flowers!

MARIE. I do, very much. As a rare delight. But like this, at every step—I don't.

PAVEL. Are you bored with me?

MARIE. With you? Why should I be? I'm bored in general. Without you I was bored, and, forgive me, with you I'm bored as well. It's not your fault—nothing to do with you.

PAVEL. Somehow I have nothing to do with your life.

MARIE. You mustn't think that way. You know very well and I know even better the role you have played in my life. You rescued me. And you did it so modestly, with such nobility, magnanimity. To this day I don't know why it was you did that.

PAVEL. When riches suddenly descended on me, I was completely at a loss. I saw them as a resource that would enable me to realize, even if only in part, those vain, those sweet and bitter daydreams that had helped me back there, in Saratov to endure shame and poverty. I didn't know a thing, hadn't seen a thing apart from deformity and malice. And then I set eyes on you—a being of an utterly different breed, not the human breed, no. And the way I first glimpsed you! Despairing, nowhere to go, out of my mind. I gave you what was needed for your salvation, but I also gave you all of myself—something of which you had no need.

MARIE. You shouldn't think like that, Pavel. Who can know what another person needs?

PAVEL. It was so unexpected! If only my fortune had come to me gradually—one ruble then two, two rubles then twenty, then a hundred, a thousand and so on. But all at once, all at once!

MARIE. I still don't know how much money you have.

PAVEL. A great deal! And then—there's you! Your love! It's the same as millions after poverty. All that beauty, all that tenderness, everything that's holy in this world . . .

MARIE. So it seems that younger brother of yours is extraordinarily good-looking?

PAVEL. Who did you hear that from?

MARIE. From you, Pavel. How funny you are!

PAVEL. Oh yes, oh yes. Sorry, I'd forgotten. So there I was, completely at a loss. And I still am. I'm always at a loss when I'm with you.

> A noisy group of young men and women descends the stairs. One of the young men is apparently leaving, he wears a traveling cloak, a hotel-boy carries a case. Everyone laughs and kisses the departing man good-bye.

YOUNG MAN. Lizzie, what is that perfume? I can never remember.
LIZZIE. *Émeraude, émeraude.* Why don't you make a note of it?
YOUNG MAN. So you'll smell of emeralds?
LIZZIE. You silly boy!

> Everyone laughs for no apparent reason. The hotel motorcar gleams at the entrance. Panes of glass in the revolving door constantly emit rainbows. The car pulls away, the horn sounding the Siegfried motif. The group goes back in. The young women glance at MARIE as they pass, and run upstairs even faster. One of the young men comes to a halt as if intending to light a cigarette; he also looks at MARIE and then slowly joins the others. All this time MARIE is persistently smelling her armful of flowers.

PAVEL. You don't have enough people around you. There are never more than the two of us, just the two.
MARIE. We do have visits from your friends and admirers.
PAVEL. No, it's not that. They are visiting me. But what about you?
MARIE. They are my friends, too.
PAVEL. But Marie, things can't go on like this! Say something. Why don't you love me?
MARIE. I do love you.
PAVEL. Say that "I love you" like someone who really does!
MARIE. I do the best I can. What is it you want?
PAVEL. What stands between us?
MARIE. Do you want to know?
PAVEL. I beg you to tell me.
MARIE. What stands between us is gratitude.

PAVEL. I don't demand that.

MARIE. But I demand it of myself, and I live as if I were a stone, a carcass. And I feel myself to be a slave.

PAVEL. Am I not your slave?

MARIE. I feel myself to be a slave.

PAVEL. And that is what prevents you from loving me?

MARIE. I can't force myself, and I don't want to, and there hasn't been time to grow to love you. It all happened so quickly.

PAVEL. You cannot forgive me because you stood on your knees in front of me?

MARIE. How stupid you are, Pavel! Stupid and rude! How could anyone possibly love you?

Enter BARON FRIEDRICH VON STEINBACH
wearing a suit that is very light in color without
being completely white. He is preceded by a hotel-
boy in a sky blue jacket.

HOTEL-BOY. Mr. Lukin, Baron von Steinbach to see you.

PAVEL. Here I am.

FRIEDRICH. You are Pavel Andreyevich Lukin?

PAVEL. How can I be of service?

FRIEDRICH. I am Baron von Steinbach from Silesia. Friedrich is my name. Forgive me for just turning up like this. Though there's really nothing to be surprised at. You are an artist. But it was not your art that drew me to you. I have been looking for you everywhere, I have traveled to your native land, I have been collecting information about you, I have been thinking about you at night. So this is what you look like! Medium height, light brown hair, straight nose; but those eyes ... of course, that's how they had to be. I had never seen a photograph of you, but I ... how can I put this? I was very close to being in love with you.

PAVEL. Did you hear about me from someone?

FRIEDRICH. From Nikifor Zhilinsky.

PAVEL. Oh, from Nikifor? He's a friend of mine.

FRIEDRICH. Who, knowing you, could fail to become your friend?

PAVEL. So what did you find out?

FRIEDRICH. Everything. Your character, your childhood, your strange fate, your ideas, your deeds. To me it all seemed like magic. As if I'd been waiting all my life for such a man!

MARIE. Pavel! It seems that you can be loved even from a distance. Let me kiss you.

Kisses him.

PAVEL. Let me introduce you: Friedrich von Steinbach. My wife.

FRIEDRICH. Your wife? This lady?

MARIE. This lady and no other. I am the wife of Pavel Andreyevich.

FRIEDRICH. Is he married?

MARIE. You managed to find out everything about him but didn't find out that he was married. What negligence!

PAVEL. It doesn't make any difference.

FRIEDRICH. May I hope that you will allow me to pay you a visit one of these days?

PAVEL. Of course, of course—come on Wednesday.

FRIEDRICH. I have the honor to take my leave.

MARIE. Do let me put a flower in your lapel. You can't walk about without a flower in Rome: the flower girls won't leave you in peace, especially with a cute little face like yours, and you'll get embarrassed, being so young. As for me, I won't be paying any attention to your face, and there's certainly no need to be embarrassed by Pavel Andreyevich's wife. Now you see how splendid you look!

FRIEDRICH (kisses her hand). Many thanks. Good-bye.

PAVEL. Until Wednesday. We are staying in suite seventeen. Come about five.

Exit FRIEDRICH.

MARIE. It'll be interesting to see which of us he'll be jealous of: you or me?

PAVEL. What nonsense! Why should he be jealous?

MARIE. It's in his nature. That's obvious straight away.

PAVEL. What's in his nature?

MARIE (singing).
>   Idealist, idealist,
>   Enthusiast, enthusiast.

So what are you looking at me like that for?

Gathers up her armful of flowers and walks toward
the elevator. Pavel follows.

5ᵗʰ Tableau

A deserted seashore. Overturned boats. Toward
evening. NERO (eleven years old) and PERTINAX.

NERO. Let's sit on these boats.

PERTINAX. We should walk a bit more, Nero, exercise is
good for you.

NERO. I'm tired, I want to sit down. Who's in whose service:
you in mine or I in yours? I pay you a salary—so you should
do what I like.

PERTINAX. I am your tutor and I am older than you—you
should obey me.

NERO. That's during lessons and when you're talking sense.
But to go for a walk or not to go for a walk—that is as I wish.

PERTINAX. And one shouldn't neglect one's health either.

NERO. All right, all right. Don't be cross. I've already sat
down. Another time I'll let you have your way, and we'll be
quits. Is there tar here? When I grow up I'm never going to
wear my clothes more than once. So that they'll always be
like new. Now you go around a whole week in the same
shirt, and then they launder it and then you have to put it
back on—it's humiliating! Tell me a story, Pertinax. It's
evening, we're sitting by the sea, and the older one is supposed to tell a story.

PERTINAX. What shall I tell you about? About the sea?

NERO. Makes no difference—about the sea if you like, although it's something I can't stand. But you must have seen
a thing or two in your day.

PERTINAX. Well, I suppose I have—but not much to serve
the cause of education.

NERO. Everything can serve the cause of education; you just
have to give it the right twist. And what do I need with education? Just tell me a story. Did you ever go to sea?

PERTINAX. Yes I did—and how many times!

NERO. Ever get sunk?

PERTINAX. No, the gods were merciful.

NERO. Too bad.

PERTINAX. Too bad I didn't get sunk?

NERO. I like it when people get sunk, when there are fires,

when there are earthquakes—something that's out-of-the-ordinary. When a tiger mauls a girl.

PERTINAX. Why a girl?

NERO. Don't know. It's more beautiful that way. So where did you travel?

PERTINAX. Well, I've been to Smyrna, to Rhodes, to Alexandria.

NERO. So what did you do, let's say in Alexandria? You're a terrible bore—can't get a word out of you. All right then, what did you do in Alexandria?

PERTINAX. I was in service.

NERO. Eternal gods, in what kind of service?

PERTINAX. In a certain house.

NERO. What sort of house? This isn't a story—it's torture.

PERTINAX. In Alexandria I served in the kind of house where only women lived.

NERO. Like ours?

PERTINAX. Not exactly. It was a merry house.

NERO. No, our house isn't a merry one.

PERTINAX. The house had many visitors.

NERO. And what's so merry about that? Auntie Lepida has visitors, but all they do is complain about their lot. If I were master of the house, I would invite conjurors. They would do tricks, and I would watch them. And then I'd invite the neighborhood boys. They would listen and praise me, then I could beat them up. Now that would be merry. All right, so what happened next? Visitors came. And the house didn't even catch fire?

PERTINAX. No.

NERO. Too bad!

PERTINAX. Then I got the sack. Didn't have a job, went hungry.

NERO. You know, that's a lousy story. We'd better go home.

6th Tableau

A backroom in a small restaurant. A stairway leads to a balcony with a door onto a landing, from which another stairway descends to the main hall. Night. Seven people whose costume is such as to arouse suspicion. Among them POMPEO and MARIANNA. MARIANNA dozes in a corner, occasionally waking. REDENTORE is an old man, ULISSO is

elderly; CARLO, POMPEO, LUIGI are adults;
CESARE and VITTORIO are teenagers.
REDENTORE divides coins and banknotes into
seven piles.

REDENTORE. There you are. Forty lire each. Don't expect
as much as a soldo before next Saturday. The Russian isn't
going to give any more.
POMPEO. He promised to come today.
REDENTORE. Did you hand him the letter?
POMPEO. That's when he promised.
LUIGI. Better if he doesn't bring his missus along.
POMPEO. Makes no difference if she's with him or not.
LUIGI. Only seems like that. For now.
ULISSO. Even the best of snakes is still a snake?
LUIGI. You've said it.
REDENTORE. Everything ready up there?
CESARE. As you ordered.
REDENTORE. Complain more about taxes.
LUIGI. What taxes? He won't believe that taxes are what
we're suffering from.
REDENTORE. He sure will. He's a Russian and doesn't un-
derstand a thing. They think heavy taxes and bans on pub-
lic demonstrations are the greatest of atrocities. And an
extra half-an-hour on the working day. For that, they're
ready for anything.
LUIGI. Is he crazy?
REDENTORE. Who can say? Makes no difference to us. For
us he's made to measure.
ULISSO. As long as he's got money.
REDENTORE. He's got enough to last us a long time.
LUIGI. Could he be an agent?
REDENTORE. Even if he is—isn't it all the same to us?
LUIGI. And by the way. That bastard has been pestering me
again with that hellish contraption of his. Ten thousand he
promised.
REDENTORE. Why don't they arrange their assassinations
themselves?
LUIGI. By using us they want to get politics out of the way.
REDENTORE. That's something we need to talk over. A dan-
gerous business and a ridiculous fee. On the other hand,
we could get something out of the turmoil. But in any case

... Where is it to be—in the Hotel Vittoria, where the Fascist delegation is putting up?

CESARE (*laughs*). You must agree to that one! A police agent came to me with the same proposition. They want to set up a provocation to entrap the anarchists. They'll pay, too.

POMPEO. And that Russian, he could be put to use, too, all the more as the hotel where he's staying ...

REDENTORE. Not a whisper to him about these propositions! This is our plan for the salvation of humanity. Main thing: complain more about taxes. Well, let's be going. He seems to be coming upstairs.

CESARE. Should I turn the light off?

REDENTORE. Leave it alone! Marianna's sleeping here, too.

CESARE. Could she have heard?

REDENTORE. Doesn't matter if she did! She's one of us.

CESARE. No trusting her, say what you like!

Everyone goes upstairs, MARIANNA jumps up.

MARIANNA. My God, what is going to happen?

Enter PAVEL.

MARIANNA. Mr. Lukin, a word with you!

PAVEL. I haven't got time, Marianna, I'm late as it is. Are the others all there?

MARIANNA. They are.

PAVEL. You see.

MARIANNA. Just a few moments.

PAVEL. Later.

MARIANNA. Later will be too late.

POMPEO comes downstairs.

POMPEO. Ah, Your Excellency, Mr. Chairman! We're all waiting for you! We've got some serious business to discuss.

PAVEL. Forgive me, I got a bit held up.

POMPEO. That's all right. (*To MARIANNA.*) What are you hanging around for? Get to bed! Be careful, Your Excellency, the third step's a bit shaky.

Exit with PAVEL.

MARIANNA. My God, what is going to happen?

Runs downstairs.

7ᵗʰ Tableau

An orchard. Thick grass. NERO (fourteen years old)
and SERVILIUS lie embraced.

SERVILIUS. There you are, Nero, nothing has happened to
you.
NERO. Oh, Servilius, it was wonderful, just like a shipwreck!
Everything started rocking, the very earth seemed to tremble, things went dark before my eyes, the blood went to my
head. Is it always like that?
SERVILIUS. Always. Of course not everyone is so sensitive.
Look at you, you're still out of breath, sweating. You're all
covered in sweat, Nero—you really are. And you're so
sweet.
NERO. I'm a gingerhead. There are lots of gingerheads in
our family, that's why we're "Enobarbi."
SERVILIUS. What does it matter if you're ginger? A little
ginger sun, that's what you are. You're a very kind, obliging
boy.
NERO. I know I am.
SERVILIUS. And a little bit plump too.
NERO. Is that a good thing?
SERVILIUS. Of course it is. Like satin pillows everywhere.
NERO. I love you, Servilius! I shall never forget you, never
leave you.
SERVILIUS. Only don't tell anyone about what happened.
We'll both get into trouble.
NERO. I understand. Servilius, is there anything wrong with
me?
SERVILIUS. What do you mean "wrong"?
NERO. Well, do I have any shortcomings?

A gang of urchins comes running into the orchard,
shouting, with watchmen in pursuit, followed by
LEPIDA, PERTINAX and maidservants.

WATCHMAN. It's locked, locked up! There's no escaping, you
little imps. Just wait till I get my hands on you—you'll rue

the day! You won't sit down for a week. If I catch some little
brat I'll give him a thrashing, but if the scamp's a bit older,
then I know what I'll do with him.

NERO. What's the matter? What's all the noise about?

LEPIDA. Again they've shaken a whole tree bare of apples.
No way of keeping them under control. Or have the watchmen grown lazy? That'll be the fifth tree they've shaken the
apples off.

NERO. And you've decided to punish them severely?

LEPIDA. After that they won't be stealing apples any more.
I'll give them something to remember. I've especially paid
a couple of our strongest fullers to give the guilty ones a
thrashing.

NERO. But what apple tree are you talking about?

LEPIDA. My favorite, the one that stands by the bathhouse—
the golden pip.

NERO. But it was me who shook it.

LEPIDA. You, Nero?

NERO. Me.

LEPIDA. Impossible.

NERO. I was the one.

WATCHMAN. What are you saying? I saw who shook it myself. Two of them there were. The first one a little nipper,
the other one much bigger than you are.

NERO. It was me who shook it!

LEPIDA (*looking at him intently*). Very well, Nero, it's you
who'll get the punishment. (*To the others.*) You can go. I'll
call you when I need you.

Exeunt except for Nero and Servilius.

SERVILIUS. Nero, surely it couldn't have been you?

NERO. It wasn't me.

SERVILIUS. And you took the blame on yourself in order to
save the guilty ones from punishment?

NERO. Yes.

SERVILIUS. That's very noble of you. A regal magnanimity.
Don't blush: it's true. You know what, when you were talking with your aunt, I thought . . . You were asking me if you
had any shortcomings. All right then, now it seems to me
that you are a bit pudgy.

NERO. What do you mean, "pudgy"? Are you trying to say I'm
a roly-poly?

SERVILIUS. I wouldn't say a roly-poly—though with that plumpness of yours, maybe you really are a bit pudgy.

NERO. Idiot! Fat lot you understand, you spindle-legged heron! I'll order your legs to be broken and your head to be scraped—so you'll end up worse off than any roly-poly! Dares to think it a good thing to be a great hulking brute! And I loved you so, trusted you so, I tried so hard to be better, to be worthy of your friendship. Traitor! Trash!

8th Tableau

The hotel garden. The windows in MARIE's room are lit up, the door onto the veranda is open. From the veranda a stairway leads down to the garden.

MARIANNA (*enters hurriedly*). There are her windows. There's light in them. They're not asleep yet. But I don't want her to notice me. I'll wait till he leaves. Surely he won't be spending the night with her.

She retreats into the shadows. FRIEDRICH comes out onto the veranda.

MARIE (*from the window*). I might have left it where we were sitting, on the bench by the fountain. Can you find your way alone? It's dark now. There's thick greenery there. Do you have a match? There's nothing really of value in the bag—doesn't matter if it gets lost.

FRIEDRICH. I'll be back in a minute. I'll find my way. Strange that Pavel Andreyevich hasn't come yet.

MARIE. It happens sometimes. You'd better wait for him. He'll be very upset if you go away. If talking to me is too much of a bore, you can play Debussy's second book of preludes. Do come back soon. Pick me a rose on the way.

Moves away from the window. FRIEDRICH goes down into the garden.

MARIANNA. Baron von Steinbach?

FRIEDRICH. Who's that?

MARIANNA. You don't know me. Never mind. The main thing is she shouldn't hear. Mr. Lukin is in danger. They are deceiving him. Thieves and bandits, that's what they are. Keep him away from the explosion.

FRIEDRICH. What explosion? I don't understand a thing.

MARIANNA. No reason why you should. Just remember to do what I say. It's all a lie; there shouldn't be any explosion. And he's not the only one who's in danger. I'm a friend. Makes no difference who. Only make sure she doesn't find out. And hurry up. This very night. Or it'll be too late.

Disappears.

MARIE (*at the window*). Friedrich, who are you talking to? You're back already. That was quick. Pavel has just telephoned to say we shouldn't wait for him. He sends you his greetings. Makes his excuses. Business affairs will delay him till morning. Come up for a half an hour anyway. It's only half past eleven. And where's that rose, and my bag? Oh, what an unchivalrous gallant you are! But then you're too young to be chivalrous.

FRIEDRICH goes in. Window and door are closed.
Music is heard.

9th Tableau

A door to LEPIDA's house. LEPIDA is sitting on the porch, a letter in her hand. She has been crying. In front of her stands a courier. Household servants surround them. NERO is in the middle of the yard.

LEPIDA. O ye gods, ye gods! Accept my gratitude for your mercy. Although I can't read, these lines are sacred to me. They bring liberty, riches and power to all our house. You've heard: Agrippina has been brought back to Rome, Nero has been confirmed as his father's heir, and has also been left a legacy by his late stepfather Crispus Passienus. And the divine Claudius promises to adopt him! When the gods are gracious they do not know human measure, their mercy is infinite! Nero, I am old now, and have grown used to the provinces. But your star is bright, and it is on the rise. Open the cupboard where the lares are kept, light the candles, bring out the sacred gruel, let a swine be slaughtered.

SERVINGMAID. Holy, holy, holy. Many years may he live, many years. Holy is the hour, holy the house, holy the place, holy the Emperor, holy is Nero. Many years may he live, many years!

SIDONIA. Look, look. An eagle is hovering over Nero's head. It is an omen.

All, including NERO, gaze into the sky.

SERVINGMAID (*in a whisper*). Holy is the hour, holy the house, holy the place, holy is Nero.

LEPIDA. Hush, let us greet it in silence.

Silence.

NERO. I cannot, I cannot remain silent any longer! Auntie, all of you—sky, eagle, gods, stones, dogs, dust, air. Hearken, hearken. I swear an oath. If the gods extend their ultimate grace, if my star take its appointed course, if I attain the heights preordained for me, I swear that everybody shall be happy; not a minute shall pass without a good deed, not a drop of blood shall be spilled. I will yield up all that I possess; I will be a merciful judge; no one shall depart from me empty-handed. My face will I hide from no one, for everyone will I dance. To everyone will I bring joy, comfort, support. The very name of Nero shall be as joyful tidings!

SERVINGMAID. Do not approach him, do not touch him. Holy the hour, holy the house, holy the place, holy is Nero.

A great flash of lightning, without thunder.

NERO. Ohhhhh! (*Loses consciousness.*)

10ᵀᴴ Tableau

An explosion. The entire stage is filled with smoke. When it clears, the hotel yard becomes visible. The building is on fire. Firefighters. Turmoil. Ladders, jets of water. Articles are dragged out. Servants run about in confusion. People at windows, screaming.

> Thieves run into the building and come running out
> with bundles. Clangor and fire alarms. In the
> foreground is a parrot in a cage: the bird's
> screeches alternate between "Fool" and "Guard!"
> Husbands and wives, mothers and children,
> brothers and sisters search for each other.
> Bright sun.

POMPEO (*at the window*). Catch, sonny boy, catch! The last of our possessions. (*Throws down an enormous bundle containing silverware, which makes a jangling sound.*)

CESARE. Got it! (*Picks up the bundle.*)

FIRST MAN. Is that your silver?

CESARE. Yes, the last of our possessions. (*Runs off with the bundle.*)

VOICES. When will there be an end to these communist outrages? The main thing for them is that none of the delegates has been harmed—eating their breakfast they were, didn't even leave the dining room. They simply finished eating, got into their cars and drove away. There's cynicism for you. They're obviously in cahoots with the police. You're breaking my arm. Sorry, I thought you were my husband. No, it seems I'm someone else. Won't be easy to put out this fire. Six units of the fire brigade. But fire isn't the worst thing! The explosion collapsed an entire wing—lopped it off like a chunk of bread. It's horrible, horrible! Even if you didn't get caught in it, your nerves are affected. Well, you know, after the imperialist war with all its horrors . . . It seems to me, there are lots of criminals around. Surely all these bums can't be putting up at this hotel. As usual, the police managed to be somewhere else.

ENGLISHMAN. This is the first time something has made a strong impression on me since the sinking of the *Titanic*.

> PAVEL appears on the roof.

VOICES. Now, what is he doing up there? How did he manage to get up there? Looks like he wants to throw himself off the roof.

MARIE (*from the window*). Bring him back! Bring him back!

PARROT. Guard!

PAVEL. Listen everyone, listen! This is the dawn of liberty. I will give you everything I have. Tidings of great joy! Tidings of great joy!

Throws down money. Some of the banknotes catch fire and continue falling.

VOICES. This is ridiculous! Stop him throwing down banknotes. Gold and silver is all he should throw. The performance is completely disorganized. Turn the jet on him.

PAVEL. Fire will purify everything. Only the naked man is free. Joy, comfort and grace. Tidings of great joy!

Throws down money.

VOICES. How long is this going on for? Until he's thrown all his money away.

POLICEMAN (to POMPEO). You're under arrest—you're Crooked Pompeo.

POMPEO. What do you mean "crooked"?

POLICEMAN. It's all the same to me. We've been looking for you. This is your handiwork.

POMPEO. What has it got to do with me? I'm small fry. Try looking a bit higher up.

POLICEMAN (looking up at the roof). Him?

POMPEO. Could be.

MARIE (walks up on FRIEDRICH's arm, to the policeman). Can't you see he's insane?

PARROT. Guard!

MARIANNA. A saint, that's what he is!

MARIE. And who can this be? I'm going mad.

FRIEDRICH. And you know you're the one who's to blame for everything.

MARIE. What do you mean—I am? You must be delirious, Friedrich. Let's run, let's run away! How horrible.

PAVEL. Tidings of great joy! Tidings of great joy!

VOICES. Turn the jet on him! He's finished throwing down money.

The jet is directed at PAVEL. He runs from one spot to another. Policemen appear on the roof.

PAVEL. Tidings of great joy!

The parrot hisses.

End of Act One.

Act II
1st Tableau

Rome. A stairway inside the palace. At the top, a
curtain is drawn. In front of it are several servants.
Early morning. Almost dark.

1ST SERVANT. I can hardly keep my eyelids apart. They
could do with propping up.

2ND SERVANT. And why has Nero taken it into his head to
keep delaying his appearance?

1ST. The auguries have not been favorable. With him everything depends on auguries. Without omens he won't take a
step.

2ND. Yes, and that's how it should be.

3RD SERVANT. Will Agrippina be with him, and Seneca?

1ST. Couldn't be any other way.

3RD. Say what you like, I'm surprised at our widow—how can
she bear to look at the body of the husband she poisoned
herself?

2ND. Won't be the first time.

1ST. Now don't you go gossiping—it's none of our business.

2ND. You're right.

3RD. Tough old fellow he was, say what you like. Toadstools
didn't work. Had to give him a poisoned enema, and even
that took its time. And Agrippina never took her eyes off
him for a moment.

2ND. I would have thrown up.

1ST. Perhaps it's all lies; he just overate and died.

3RD. A likely story! So why did they keep his death secret for
so long? It was Friday he died, you know—and what is it
today? Just think about it. Edicts were proclaimed, de-
crees were signed, actors were brought in to cheer him up.
But long before that, all he was in a condition to do was to
stink out the whole palace.

4TH SERVANT (*running in from below*). Hurry up! Hurry up!
They're coming . . .

Servants run off. Enter senators, who assemble in
an orderly fashion. NERO (seventeen years old)
appears below, together with AGRIPPINA and
SENECA. They are in mourning. In front of the
senators they come to a halt.

SENATORS. Long life to Emperor Domitius Claudius Nero. May the gods preserve you, O chaste Nero. Most benign Nero, may the gods preserve you; O merciful Nero, may the gods preserve you. Upholder of grace, fount of wisdom, prop of the oppressed, defense of the virtuous, shield of the fatherland, terror of the foe, pillar of the law, solace of humanity, glory of eternal Rome, ever-radiant star, our guiding star. Refuge of the distressed, scion of the great mother, father of his loving subjects. Long life to you (*three times*).

NERO. Only you mustn't call me the father of my subjects. They'll think I'm eighty years old. It ages me.

SENATORS. Pay due respect to the body of your father, O sovereign.

> The senators make way. The curtain is drawn aside. The body of Claudius is displayed on a ceremonial litter. NERO, AGRIPPINA and SENECA ascend the staircase and take their leave of the body. They descend.

CAPTAIN OF THE GUARD. What password do you assign for the day?

NERO. Best of Mothers.

2ND Tableau

> Circus entrance. Toward evening. A crowd.

SCRAPS OF CONVERSATION. What are you waiting for?
The Emperor's return.
We were sent to make sure he'd see a crowd at the entrance.
Long time we had to wait!
Yes, it's ten hours we've been waiting.
And he's still singing?
Still is.
May the gods grant him health. And the audience isn't dispersing yet?
The doors were locked as soon as he began singing.
Ever heard him sing?
Just once, in the palace garden. I happened to be riding by.
They say he's not bad.
His voice is lacking in volume—but isn't bad for an amateur.

Better be careful. Someone might overhear.
It goes on and on.
Good thing people stocked up with provisions.

> A man is carried out of a side entrance and
> deposited on the ground. He jumps to his feet.

MAN. Ooof! Managed to get out somehow. There'd have been
no letting me out if I hadn't put on an act of sudden death.
1ST CITIZEN. So you haven't really given up the ghost? Let's
give him a beating, lads! (*MAN runs away.*)
2ND. They say one woman gave birth in the circus.
1ST. Why did she go to the circus at the last minute?
3RD. Interesting, all the same. The Emperor gave both mother
and child their freedom there and then.
VOICES. Quiet! The show's over. The Emperor is coming out.

> Doors swing open. Procession. Preceding NERO, a
> policeman carries a lyre. Nero wears a garland of
> gold. His mouth is covered by a scarf.

All hail! All hail!
Why is the lyre being carried by a policeman?
Pride, you can be sure of that.
Stop talking rubbish! The Emperor does everything accord-
ing to the rules, he even draws lots the same as everyone
else.
What's he all wrapped up for? Is he ill?
He's afraid of a cold in his throat.
Look, he wants to say something.
Why doesn't he use his own voice, then?
He never speaks to the people.
All hail, All hail!
Who are those fellows, all wearing the same shirt?
What fellows?
The ones with the bracelets on their left arm, with the long
hair?
Those are the appraisers. They are the first to give the signal
for enthusiasm.
All hail! All hail!
TOWN CRIER. Citizens, the Emperor is pleased to grant the
wishes of those who didn't have the opportunity to gain
entry to the circus, and for them he will sing a ditty. (*NERO*

*whispers to his immediate neighbor, he to the next man, and so
on until the message reaches the town crier.)* Ah, very well.
The Emperor craves your indulgence. He has just given a
long performance. (*The same operation.*) The Emperor will
now sing an anacreontic ditty—the epic having been per-
formed in there.
CLAQUE. Bravo, bravo, bravo, bravo!
TOWN CRIER. Attention, attention.
CLAQUE. Bravo, bravo, bravo, bravo!

> NERO prepares for his performance, unwrapping
> his throat, taking and tuning his lyre. He smiles,
> clears his throat.

CLAQUE. Bravo, bravo, bravo, bravo!
NERO (*sings*).
> A man who ever roams the sea
> In search of vain, delusive profit,
> And, rich at last, can only die,
> The naked thing that he was born.
> Another brandishes a sword
> A stagnant puddle is his potion,
> He slumbers shod on harsh campaigns,
> And sees his home but in his dreams.
> A third has no delight but Chloe,
> Obedient to her idle whim—
> But let capricious Zephyr puff
> And where is Chloe? Not a trace.
> Another fate have I elected,
> My profit is the people's rapture,
> Song my hardest fought campaign,
> Devoted spouse to me my lyre.

CLAQUE. Bravo, bravo, bravo, bravo!
Why is he hoarse? Can't make out a word.
Bravo, bravo, bravo, bravo!

> They throw garlands, release birds from cages,
> spread kerchiefs and cloaks on the ground.

NERO. There's no pleasing everyone! Such is the lot of an
artist. (*Withdraws.*)

> Long live the Emperor! Long live the Emperor!

3rd Tableau

Five years before Act One.
Saratov. A room in the house of the Ivolgins. PAVEL
(twenty-five years old). NIKIFOR ZHILINSKY.

ZHILINSKY. So you've never even seen him?

PAVEL. Never. At first I was very eager to see what he looked
like. Even in a dream. Going to sleep, I'd concentrate all
my thoughts on him. It didn't work. I did dream of him
once; he looked like our parish priest, but in hussar uni-
form. I was terribly upset. Since then I've stopped wanting
to see him, even in real life.

ZHILINSKY. You don't even have a picture or something?

PAVEL. Mother didn't have any. Didn't care for them. She
probably destroyed them.

ZHILINSKY. A strange man, say what you like.

PAVEL. Sometimes I'm afraid of him, sometimes I think I can
manage to understand him. But these days I don't often
think of him.

ZHILINSKY. How could he have let your mother almost
starve to death? And your sister too.

PAVEL. He isn't my sister's father. She's older than I am. And
anyway, Mama didn't want to live. If it hadn't been starvation, she'd have found some other way. A kind of suicide.
In a way I was even pleased it happened like that.

ZHILINSKY. But surely you loved your mother?

PAVEL. Yes, I did love her. But that's just why I was angry
with her—and because I couldn't change anything. The
two of them tormented me. And father, you know, he
wouldn't send us anything. His revenge maybe, I don't
know. They used to complain all the time, and it got me
down.

ZHILINSKY. And now?

PAVEL. You know all about that. Father sends a few pennies
from time to time. And to the Ivolgins, rather than to me
direct. He thinks I'm still a five-year-old. Maybe he's afraid
of seeming old.

ZHILINSKY. Of course he is tremendously wealthy. Everyone knows that.

PAVEL. Unfortunately. The Ivolgins know, and I know. There
must be some plan behind his actions: not a word from him
until the death of Mama. I did use to write to him as a

child—a letter on his name day, one to wish him a happy new year. He never answered, not even once. And then this banishment to Saratov, to the Ivolgins, and the tiny amounts he sends. As if he wanted to make me endure poverty and humiliation.

ZHILINSKY. I don't think it was all so carefully calculated.

PAVEL. If it wasn't, then it's just too absurd.

ZHILINSKY. And what about you, Pavel? You do remember our plans?

PAVEL. What else do you think is keeping me alive?

ZHILINSKY. But just look at yourself—it's as if you haven't woken up. Of course, the Ivolgins are incredibly bourgeois but I can't help asking the same question as they do: why don't you do anything?

PAVEL. I write. You know that yourself. You're taken up with your medicine, I with my writing. But with medicine somehow you know exactly what you're going to be doing. You get your diploma, then you start work at the hospital, then you set up a practice. But with writing there aren't any such stages. The way the Ivolgins see it, a writer isn't someone who writes, but someone who gets into print—as if he belonged to some kind of handicraft guild. They're right, of course. But to me it's disgusting.

ZHILINSKY. And what else?

PAVEL. What else? I'm waiting.

ZHILINSKY. What for?

PAVEL. I don't know.

ZHILINSKY. For your father's death?

PAVEL. No, no, no!

Enter IVOLGINA.

IVOLGINA. Why are you shouting like that, Pavel—you're not in the street. And you, Zhilinsky, you're always hanging about our place! Five times a day you show up. In the morning, at lunchtime, and at night. Hours don't exist for you. You should get it into your head that Sonya is a young lady who has come of age, that it's hardly proper for a man who isn't one of the family to be in the house. Seems I've already talked to you about that. Are you entirely devoid of self-respect? Another man would be ashamed.

PAVEL. Lizaveta Nikolayevna!

IVOLGINA. I've been Lizaveta Nikolayevna for forty-five
years. Time you thought up something else.

PAVEL. This is my room, you get paid for it, and I can receive
whomever I please, and for as long as I please. And I must
ask you to remove yourself.

ZHILINSKY. It isn't worth it, Pavel—I was just about to leave
anyway.

PAVEL. I'm asking you to remove yourself.

IVOLGINA. Is that meant for me? Snotty-nosed pup.

PAVEL. Pups with snotty noses don't exist.

IVOLGINA. Take a look in the mirror—and you'll see that
they do.

PAVEL. This is getting absolutely ridiculous.

Enter SONYA.

SONYA. Mama, sugar first then water, or water first then
sugar?

IVOLGINA. I'll make it myself right away. I've forgotten what
I came for!

ZHILINSKY. Good day, Sofia Platonovna.

SONYA. Good day indeed—five times a day you "good-day"
me. Oh, Pavel, your goddess is about to come riding by any
minute.

PAVEL. What goddess?

SONYA. There's only one goddess in these parts—Maria Petrovna, Miss Rublyova.

PAVEL. Marie? You're making it up.

SONYA. As if I'd bother! I saw from the kitchen that their
cavalcade had deigned to take the Volskaya Street turn—
they should be riding past our windows this very moment.

PAVEL. It's raining.

ZHILINSKY (*at the window*). The rain has stopped.

PAVEL (*going over to the window*). There's a rainbow over
there!

IVOLGINA. You'd better comb that mop of yours!

4th Tableau

A small yard within the palace, NERO is lying on
his back, his arms wide-stretched; there is a sheet
of lead on his chest. Above him a lilac-colored
awning. Nearby—DOCTOR, SPORUS and a few

attendants. SPORUS, who is wearing a curly, dark
blue wig is painted like a doll, with eyes of an
intense sky blue. DOCTOR is looking at a sundial.

DOCTOR. Twenty minutes of complete immobility is required. Don't answer . . . Silence is essential. As they pass
through lilac tinted cloth the sun's rays acquire a special
healing property. Lead regulates the distribution of adi-
pose tissue. Good, good.

A pregnant POPPAEA enters with a sumptuous
retinue; directly behind her is a bedizened monkey
that constantly mimics her gestures.

POPPAEA. And that is the emperor. Take a good look. Did I
divorce my first husband to get a buffoon for a second?
What are you doing, Nero? Get rid of all these flatterers
and swindlers, don't disgrace yourself, and be a man if not
an emperor. Be a Roman.

NERO shakes his fist at her.

DOCTOR. Careful now, Emperor—no movement.
POPPAEA. I'm not talking about the nightly escapades that
not only demean your dignity and stain my honor, but ex-
pose your very life to danger. (*The monkey mimics her oratorical gestures.*) To play at dice with disreputable rascals,
to frequent low dives, to wreck wretched taverns, to beat
up policemen—and for what reward? The bought praises
your hangers-on lavish on the young emperor's "mettle-
some spirit." Your youth will pass very quickly, Nero, and
there's no holding it back with freak shows. It's not for your
youth that you'll live in the pages of history. Neither will
you immortalize yourself with your singing. What's the
point of these ridiculous attempts to be a professional? Do
you really have so much time on your hands that you don't
know what to do with it? Of course, no one would dare to
tell you—but your last performance at the circus was pre-
posterous. I didn't know where to look.

NERO leaps to his feet, casting off the sheet of lead
with a crash. He kicks POPPAEA in the abdomen

three times. As he raises his foot, his slipper falls to
the floor. The monkey kicks SPORUS in the belly;
he guffaws.

NERO. Out! Out!! Out!!!

POPPAEA's retinue leads her off in disarray. NERO
attempts to put his slipper back on, failing at first to
find it with his bare foot. He sinks heavily into an
armchair.

NERO. Disgusting bitch! She knows very well that at present
I have been prescribed total immobility and silence and
along she comes with her reproaches. I'll bet it was Seneca
who compiled that wad of balderdash for her. Why doesn't
he open those veins of his, since he's above mere human
suffering and despises mortality? Old dotard! There just
aren't any decent people around. Only when you become
emperor do you grasp that. Power destroys all illusions.
Scum! She really has upset me—and it looks like my voice
is going again. And you, what's that long face for? You look
as if you'd swallowed a lemon.
DOCTOR. Pardon me, divine one, your deeds are ever righteous and just, but I fear that ill may come of your blow to
the Empress, bearing in mind her condition.
NERO. So much the better—she won't keep poking her nose
into things that don't concern her. On the other hand, you
may have a point. Go to her, find out how she is. Take necessary measures. Remember, you answer with your life for
her health and for that of the child. Tell her I'm sorry I lost
my temper a little. Tell her to take care of herself. If she
has any requests, let them be granted at once. Yes . . . tell
her that as long as she is pregnant, until she is delivered of
the child, I promise to give up my nocturnal strolls. Get
some flowers from the gardener for her. Off with you.

Exit DOCTOR.

NERO. Was it three times that I kicked her?
SPORUS. The monkey kicked me three times, and in the
belly, too.
COURTIER. That won't do you any harm, Sporus. Of course,

you're also an empress of sorts, but fortunately you're not pregnant—and pretty unlikely to become so.

NERO. What vulgarity! Who are you anyway? Where do you come from? You shrimp! You louse! Arrest him! Ah, ah, ah! (*Breathing heavily.*) Even in my own home, in the bosom of my family, I cannot rest assured that my desires, my tastes, my habits, my commands will not be subjected to ridicule. Arrest him. I'll let you know how he's to be dealt with. It seems that everyone is conspiring to ruin my day (*fanning himself with the flaps of his nightgown*).

2ND COURTIER. Will you be hearing reports today?

NERO. Of course, of course. The hour has come, it seems. Let them be brought in. I'll be receiving here: too much bother to move. In heat like this, I'll be receiving them in my swimming pool. I shall be swimming, so let them swim, too. Let them in. Such, Sporus, is the day of the lord of the universe. But hatters and shoemakers imagine that all Nero does is to stuff himself and crawl from one mistress to another. Their idea of imperial power. My head is sometimes crammed to bursting with affairs of state.

Enter ministers, TREASURER and ARCHITECT.

ALL. Hail to the divine Caesar Domitius Claudius Nero! May the gods preserve him, and may his day be holy and crowned with success.

NERO. Good day, gentlemen. Well, what do you have? (*To ARCHITECT.*) I see, I see: you've got a plan for the palace ready; I praise your promptness. Show it to me.

ARCHITECT unrolls a large scroll.

NERO. Very neat work, my fine fellow! Go ahead then, give me some explanation of these markings! What, for example, is that?

ARCHITECT. These here are little groves. They are scattered along the edge of a large pool. It is proposed to put tame animals in them. Everything is connected, as you can see, by means of various constructions. A complete promenade can be made under a single roof. Here is the main residence. This is the portico, this is a triple row of columns. And there are the meadows. Sitting in the summer dining room, you'll get a view of the golden fruit of Ceres.

The walls are painted with frescoes: hunting, fishing, fowl-runs and mine-works. This small chamber here is trimmed with gold throughout. Gold isn't everywhere, but concentrated in a single spot—that way it'll be more exquisite. This passageway leads to an underground labyrinth. Here is the garden exit. The central room rotates, just as the sun god does. The ceiling can be extended.

NERO. And how will that be contrived?

ARCHITECT. It's very simple. A row of joined ivory plates, each sliding behind the next, thus forming apertures for fresh air or in order to strew flowers over those present. Or the ceiling can be removed entirely.

NERO. Very good. You have taste. At last I shall live like a human being.

ARCHITECT. In this way the Palatine will be connected with the Aquiline. Four city blocks will have to be demolished for that purpose.

NERO. Naturally. It's not worth talking about. Very good. My thanks to you. And how are things proceeding with the rebuilding of houses—is everything going smoothly?

ARCHITECT. Anti-fire awnings have been installed in many places, but not everywhere. Some householders are opposed to this innovation, pleading insufficiency of means.

NERO. A lame excuse. They'll have to be fined. I hardly have the time to explain matters to each and every corn-chandler. It was laid out clearly enough in the edict. If someone failed to understand, let him blame his own stupidity.

TREASURER. May I venture to report that the treasury is very low in funds. Only enough for essential expenditures.

NERO. You're always making these terribly boring reports. No funds. So some will have to be obtained. That's what you're treasurer for.

TREASUERER. May I venture to inquire: where are they to be obtained?

NERO. Well, we can raise taxes, take a percentage of every legacy.

TREASURER. May I venture to report...

NERO. Enough of this "may I venture to report." You're getting on my nerves. Speak simply.

TREASURER. You yourself lowered taxes.

NERO. So much the better: I was the one who lowered them, and I'll be the one to raise them. After all, it's not myself I'm spending money on. It's civic improvements I'm taking care of. My plans are known to you: everything is calculated to be spread over a four-year period. If all these measures are carried out methodically and with precision, by the time four years have elapsed we will have mended all social ills: famine, epidemics, conflagrations, poverty—we will bridle the very elements. This plan is an achievement, a victory in itself.

MINISTER. But at the same time reports are coming from the northern provinces of widespread disorder—even rioting—as a direct result of the bad harvest.

NERO. Ridiculous people. Can't wait four years! Experiments with ivory powder as a fertilizer have produced absolutely marvelous results. Fertility has increased twenty-fold. Twenty-fold! They sowed half an acre and the harvest was twenty times the norm.

MINISTER. Yes, but now they say they are dying of hunger.

NERO. They say all sorts of things. Lack of discipline—that's what it is. I hear there are people in India whose self-control is such that they can go without food for three years. We have simply let ourselves go.

TREASUERER. May I venture to report . . .

NERO. There he goes again. I know what you're going to venture to report—that we are out of funds. Surely they can be obtained somewhere. Take the gold statues and vessels out of the temples and melt them down for coinage.

MINISTER. Won't you be accused of sacrilege?

NERO. Why? Reverence for the gods doesn't depend on the material from which their images are made. That's obvious. Every country, every province has its own gods, and they have their own images. That makes no difference to their essence. Here is a genuine image of a divinity for me. (*He draws a doll from his bosom.*) As you can see, it's a little girl. Who can she be? Cybele, Cora, Aphrodite, Hecate—who can tell? Or perhaps it's modeled on an ordinary little girl from Corinth. She used to run, to laugh, to love, to sell violets—and she died as we all will. But now she is Nero's guardian. I got her in a very strange way: there was terrible darkness, and the crickets were chirping. I didn't know who the passerby was. He called me by my name and gave me this doll. He said that as long as she was with me, success would be mine. And he told no lie. I named her Tyukhe. Does it really matter what name a man gives to his good fortune? Look how she's reaching out her little hand,

look how she's smiling. She won't deceive. And all she's
made of is simple clay.
TREASURER. It would be a good thing if she would help you
fill the treasury.

Enter SLAVE.

SLAVE. Emperor, some kind of foreigner seeks audience. He
first came this morning, but I didn't let him in.
NERO. Bring him in.

AFRICAN enters and prostrates himself.

NERO. Rise. Speak. What do you want?
AFRICAN. To reveal to you a mystery. To you alone.
NERO (to the others). Step back, all of you. (To AFRICAN.)
Speak.
AFRICAN. Divine one, it is fitting that you should know. A
great mystery. I know the place where Queen Dido's untold
treasures are hidden.
NERO. Beware of lying.
AFRICAN (baring his chest). Smite me if I lie.
NERO (clapping his hands). Listen, you tedious old skeptics.
He will reveal to me Dido's hidden treasures! Dido's hid-
den treasures! We are saved! Nero is saved! Rome is saved!
Oh my darling little girl! My little grey Tyukhe! (He lifts the
doll in the air and gazes at it adoringly.)

5th Tableau

A bank of the Volga. Thick bushes. Something
reminiscent of "Stenka Razin" is being sung in the
distance. Enter ZHILINSKY and PAVEL.

PAVEL. Go back to them, Nikifor, or they won't leave me
alone. I'll lie here for a bit. I simply can't take any more of
that bunch.
ZHILINSKY. It's your nerves. All right then, I'll go. Only
don't take it into your head to drown yourself.
PAVEL. What nonsense. I'll be there in half an hour.

Exit ZHILINSKY.

PAVEL. What a life! And I'll soon be twenty-five.

> Enter MARIE on horseback, at a fast pace.

MARIE. Would you hold my horse for me?

> PAVEL restrains the horse. He helps MARIE
> dismount, then hitches the horse.

Let her stand for a while. The train gave her a scare. She's a good horse, but isn't long from the estate. Good job you happened to be here. She might have carried me into the river.
PAVEL. The bank is rather steep. Could have ended badly. Sit down on my coat.

> MARIE sits down.

MARIE. I often run into you, Lukin.
PAVEL. You know who I am?
MARIE. Everyone knows everyone else here.
PAVEL. I always do my best to cross your path somehow—I've been looking for an excuse to meet you.
MARIE. That's by no means a simple proposition. We are not acquainted. And scarcely could be.
PAVEL. Well, of course, your father is Vice-Governor.
MARIE. Irony is inappropriate. That is the essential reason. We have a different circle of friends, our interests differ. What could you do at our place? It would be strange. If I were in love with you, I might well permit myself even greater eccentricities. But I'm not.
PAVEL. Whatever happens, this conversation is unlikely to be repeated. I do love you, Maria Petrovna, I love you as only a creature of this earth can love. I don't demand anything. It's enough for me just occasionally to see you—that slanting left eyebrow of yours, those quivering nostrils. When you went to Switzerland last spring, I kept trying to imagine your life there. Skating on round lakes, strolling through meadows full of grazing cows. And in the distance—always snow. I imagined you alone, without that pack of army officers—and my mind was at rest. If this world didn't have you in it, I'd go mad, as if time had been annihilated or the sun extinguished.
MARIE. Seven, only seven!

PAVEL. What do you mean, seven?

MARIE. I was counting the cuckoo's calls. I have seven more years to live. So you're in love with me. And ready, of course, to do anything to prove it.

PAVEL. I am ready to prove it—but why "of course"?

MARIE. Fetch me this whip then. (*She flings her whip into the water. PAVEL jumps from the steep bank.*)

Bravo, bravo. No, no—not with your hands. With your teeth, like a poodle. What a funny man you are. How old are you?

PAVEL, soaking wet, with the whip between his
teeth.

Ugh, how wet you are. Don't come near me. Lay the whip on the grass, wipe it dry. I'll pick it up myself. Terribly funny and very strange. You know, so strange that I'm prepared to give you a kiss. Just as in *La belle Hélène, puisque ça n'est qu'un rêve.*

PAVEL. I've never seen *La belle Hélène.*

MARIE. You poor thing. Well, pucker up your lips for me. No hands. Ugh, how wet you are. There you are then. (*Kisses him.*) This kiss is like a stone thrown into water. Just once, and lost forever. If I were a passionate lady, I would let a lackey in for the night. (*A silence.*) Lukin, why don't you take offence at "lackey"?

PAVEL. That's exactly what you wanted me to do.

MARIE. You've guessed wrong. But a man devoid of self-esteem cannot make any impression.

PAVEL. I'm not trying to make an impression, I love you.

MARIE. How old are you?

PAVEL. Twenty-five.

MARIE. I thought you were much younger. Why don't you do anything, why do you just keep hanging around the necks of those disgusting Ivolgins?

PAVEL. I write, I am preparing myself. I have a very rich father, if that interests you.

MARIE. Not particularly. Anyway, it's not your father but you who are in love with me. What have his hoards got to do with it? But you know, Lukin, I do feel a bit sorry you can't come and visit us. I could talk to you. I never talk to anyone—I play the capricious miss, the coquette, I order people about, I agree or disagree—but I never talk to anyone.

PAVEL. That's no life you're living, Maria Petrovna.

MARIE. That's too big a question, Lukin, who is living a life and who isn't. Good-bye, then. Don't be cross about "lackey."

PAVEL. I'm not cross. You will be ashamed yourself when you recall this incident.

MARIE. I never will. That I guarantee. Well, would you take me to my horse and help me mount? Ugh, how wet you are.

Exeunt.

6th Tableau
A fire.

7th Tableau

The dining room at the Ivolgins. IVOLGINA,
SONYA, and some kind of servingmaid are running
from one door to another. Windows are open onto
the front garden.

IVOLGINA. Have you ironed Pavel Andreyevich's shirt? He likes his collar well ironed. Why hasn't the milkman come? O my goodness, goodness me! Get a move on! Why does everyone seem so drowsy?

MAID. There'll be time enough to get things done.

SONYA. You'd better take care of the pie, Mama. We'll get things in order ourselves. I'll go and pick some lilac.

IVOLGINA. Yes, lilac! Is Pavel Andreyevich a young lady or something? As if he'd never seen lilac before! Maybe you could even get something from the Smetanins' greenhouse?

SONYA. People like a bit of attention.

MAID. No use crying over spilt milk!

IVOLGINA. This dummy here can't keep her nose out of things! Oh, my goodness, goodness me. We'll have to lock up the dog. Only the other day Pavel Andreyevich was saying: "What a disgusting mongrel!"

MAID. You'd do better to lock yourself up, and in the privy, too.

SONYA. And you'd do better to hold your tongue!

IVOLGINA. A ring at the door! Who on earth could that be? They've smelled it out, they've smelled it out!

SONYA. It's only Zhilinsky!

IVOLGINA. That's all right, he's one of the family.

Enter ZHILINSKY.

Have you heard about Pavel's good fortune, Nikifor Ivanovich? It must be true that, as folk say, God looks after orphans.
And I'll tell you straight that he deserves it—aren't many
such goodhearted young fellows as him about.

ZHILINSKY. I haven't seen Pavel yet, but the whole town is
talking about that legacy.

IVOLGINA. Such tittle-tattle. You'd think you were living in
a village. And what business is it of theirs?

ZHILINSKY. What's so extraordinary about that? Everything
is quite fair. The younger brother has been very well provided for. And all the rest goes to Pavel Andreyevich. He's
a love child—say what you like. And not a kopeck for anyone else. Pavel Andreyevich understands very well who
deserves to be rewarded. Who has been a friend to him
and who hasn't, who is dear to him, and who a stranger.
Whose family it was that took him in like a son, who it was
took good care of him.

SONYA laughs.

IVOLGINA. What's up with you?

SONYA. I bet the Rublyov girl is gritting her teeth.

ZHILINSKY. I've heard they've suffered some kind of misfortune.

SONYA. Daddy was caught lining his own pockets.

IVOLGINA. He was filching government funds. An investiga-
tory commission came, and a hundred thousand was missing. They arrested him, naturally.

ZHILINSKY. Maria Petrovna, too?

IVOLGINA. No. What has Maria Petrovna got to do with it?

ZHILINSKY. But surely Pyotr Prokhorovich could have
plugged the hole with money of his own?

IVOLGINA. What kind of "money of his own"? They don't
have a thing apart from his salary, and their vice-gubernatorial apartment. That they used to live in luxury doesn't
mean anything.

SONYA. Just show.

ZHILINSKY. Does Pavel know about it?

IVOLGINA. How could he not know when the whole town is abuzz with nothing else? And Pyotr Prokhorovich was taken away under police guard right before our very eyes.

ZHILINSKY. So where is Pavel now?

IVOLGINA. In the front garden. This kind of change must have disturbed him. He's such a sensitive soul.

ZHILINSKY. I'll go fetch him.

IVOLGINA. Just give him a shout from the window. Time for breakfast anyway.

ZHILINSKY (*at the window*). Pavel! Pavel! No, there's no sign of him. He must have gone somewhere. Pavel! Pavel!

SONYA. He's gone running to her!

IVOLGINA. Sonya, you'll be the death of me!

SONYA. Yes, to her, of course—to her rescue.

IVOLGINA. Nikifor Ivanovich, my dear, just you run along and bring him back. Or he'll give her all the money.

ZHILINSKY. But the money's all in the bank. How can he give it away? He has received only a tiny sum.

IVOLGINA. He'll get it out of the bank. He'll find some way to do that. Run, beg him not to. Call a policeman. He could be put in a madhouse for that! Oh my goodness, goodness me!

SONYA. Yes, seriously, Zhilinsky, do go and get hold of him. Who knows what might happen?

ZHILINSKY. All right, I'll go if you like.

IVOLGINA. Thank you for that. He's a real friend, that's clear.

Exit ZHILINSKY.

IVOLGINA (*shouts from the window*). Take the alleyway! It's closer, and isn't so baking hot.

8ᵗʰ Tableau

A room in PHAON's country retreat. NERO, PHAON, SPORUS and ACTEA are seated on a bench.

NERO. Phaon, yours is the sad privilege of seeing the Emperor in a moment of weakness, desolation. No one must know of this. Thus you enter the narrow circle of close confidants before whom Nero is not ashamed to be neither emperor nor actor, but a man. You, too, Sporus, and this quiet girl here. I do have a wet nurse, too, but she's only to take care of my childish needs.

PHAON. Whatever you may do, Emperor, I will remain grateful to you. Only by your grace do I live. You gave me freedom, well-being and tranquility. This house, everything within it, I myself—are all at your service.

NERO. Doctors say that nightmares and hallucinations result from an overfull stomach. You know how temperate I usually am. Like all singers and stage performers, I maintain a diet, am careful with the wine. It is a fragile thing, the human apparatus. So there cannot possibly be any talk of overeating. The trouble is, I am haunted by the late Poppaea. She is pregnant, as she was then, with an enormous belly—bigger than what you see in real life—and with a sick baby in her arms. Its face is just like yours, Sporus. The same blue eyes—you know, you look like Poppaea, I never noticed that before. She is walking silently along the shore, and her every step seems to reproach me—every single fold of her dress, the very slowness of her gait. At the same moment, Agrippina comes swimming out of the water and crawls onto the shore—the way she did then, when her boat sank and she saved her life by swimming. I kiss her and say: "Ugh, how wet you are." And a third woman, one I've never set eyes on before, comes running from behind a sand dune. A redhead she is, and very disheveled. In a servile manner she wipes the water from Agrippina's face, and then she pulls from her bosom a purple-painted egg, holds it out to me, and says: "Christ is risen." I didn't take it, I assure you I didn't. Maybe she's a dead woman, too, and she would have led me into a blind alley. I'm afraid of narrow corridors, always was afraid . . .

ACTEA. Perhaps you, too, will be touched by grace.

NERO. Enough of that. I know what you have in mind. No, I was wondering why it is that gratitude weighs so heavy, why it is that to benefit humanity you shouldn't do good to anyone in particular!

PHAON. Maybe it's the same as with clowns or comedians— they're a miserable lot offstage. All their cheerfulness goes into their art. Perhaps love of humanity works the same way.

ACTEA. There cannot be any real love outside the teaching of Christ.

NERO. Enough of that. Don't put any hope in my moment of weakness. I remember perfectly the rubbish you were telling me about that sect of yours. It's nothing but an ignorant mishmash of all kinds of beliefs. What's new in it is only suited to the strong, to those of high rank. Nero could be a Christian because he can afford to be one. Humbug and playacting—that's all there is to it. Anyway, that mob of yours—they are trash. Idlers and sneaks hanging on to one another for support, every one of them is a null outside the collective. They're always trying to set up a state within the state. They're prone to such cowardly misdemeanors as deceit, thievery and cheating—always in hope of pardon. Irresponsible people.

ACTEA. You do not know them, Nero.

NERO. Committing crimes, breaking laws, violating nature is something only Oedipuses can do, and to them it is given to solve the riddle of the Sphinx. Not everyone can do that. Only a man endowed with supreme power. He can do everything, he must be able to do everything.

ACTEA. But can you bring a dead man back to life?

NERO. No one can do that. Show me such a man.

ACTEA. And will you bow down before him?

NERO. I will crucify him! Lest there be temptation.

ACTEA. Antichrist! Antichrist!

NERO. No, Actea. That's too petty for me. Nero cannot set himself against a rabbi from the boondocks. You have to keep a sense of proportion. Let's talk no more about it. Don't be angry, I know you are devoted to me.

SPORUS. Emperor, let's go boating, let's catch fish in golden nets, let's teach dogs to do tricks, let's see if the seventeenth rosebush has burst into bloom, let's do something.

NERO. The wind has dropped, and the calm sea is of a transparent azure. Sea, calm, azure—everything is in your dear eyes. Your suggestion is as uncomplicated as you are yourself, but in its own way it does make sense. Let's be off.

Exeunt.

9th Tableau

The Rublyovs' house. MARIE is on her knees before PAVEL. She kisses his hand.

PAVEL. What are you doing, Maria Petrovna? What's this for?

MARIE. It's what I must do. For the first time I see a man so noble, so pure, so naïve.

PAVEL. What are you talking about? I love you, Maria Petrovna. And now I have a lot of money. Why shouldn't I help you out in your misfortune?

MARIE. I so insulted you.

PAVEL. It was perfectly natural. What was I in your eyes? Some kind of presumptuous nonentity.

MARIE. No, no. I simply hadn't understood you . . .

PAVEL. And how could you have understood me?

MARIE. I didn't . . .

PAVEL. And didn't want to either.

MARIE. Don't torment me. But no, do—bring back the past, reproach me. It's what I deserve, and you have the right to execute me.

PAVEL. Maria Petrovna, get this into your head once and for all: I do not have any right over you—and do not intend to. Everything has turned out unexpectedly, perhaps, but in a perfectly natural way. I love you now as I loved you before. I haven't changed. You may have changed toward me, but nothing follows from that. You're upset, you're over-wrought, you're unable to account for your own feelings. We'll talk about it later.

MARIE. Now, in the future, forever—I'll say it again—my life belongs to you.

PAVEL. And you won't regret that?

MARIE. No! No!

PAVEL. Perhaps you're not well, perhaps you have a fever.

MARIE. You refuse?

PAVEL. How could I? Your life belongs to me, you said? And you yourself?

MARIE. And I myself.

PAVEL. And your heart, too?

MARIE. And my heart, too.

PAVEL. And your father won't have anything against it?

MARIE. I don't think he will. Only we'll go abroad immediately, Pavel. You'll finish your play there. You really are a man of talent—with a heart like yours, it's impossible not to be talented. And now you have the means that will make it easier for you to win fame. I will always be at your side. You will see what a splendid destiny awaits us.

PAVEL. Wait, Marie. My head is going round.
MARIE. Not as fast as it's going to, my dearest genius.

She kisses him.

10ᵗʰ Tableau

Ostia. A ship stands at anchor. Statue of Nero.
Entrance to an eating place. Pinned to the wall is a
decree. Evening. A crowd.

CROWD.
We want bread! We want bread!
We want circuses! We want circuses! We want circuses!
We want bread and circuses!
VOICES.
Just read about the rations we've been allotted for to-
    morrow.
They've been reduced again.
Bastards! I bet they're stuffing themselves.
And the yids are driving up prices.
YOUNG MAN (*to elderly man*). Listen. Let's go. Only two steps
    from here you can get an excellent dinner. And it's not ex-
    pensive either. Only no one must see us. I'll come with you,
    if you like. You'll have a most enjoyable evening, that I can
    assure you.

Exeunt.

VOICES. We want bread! We want bread!
And is anything else written up there?

Someone sings:

If bread is scarce, don't worry,
To oysters we will switch.
No ready cash? We're sorry.
The temple gold will make us rich.

Neat! That's real neat! Sacrilegious scoundrel! Arsonist! Par-
ricide!
A VOICE. Remember how killingly funny Datus was in the
    atellan: "Farewell Papa! Farewell Mama!" And he made a

gesture with his hand—snip—everyone got the point. And the Emperor was in the theater, too. Didn't say a word.

ANOTHER. But Datus got deported—just like Isidorus the Cynic.

ANOTHER. Deported? You call that punishment?

We want bread! We want bread! We want bread!

> Gleaming with lanterns, a boat with revelers on board comes sailing in. They stagger ashore, singing, their arms about each other.

> Who hasn't loved, will love tomorrow,
> Will love tomorrow, who hasn't loved!

VOICES. Now those aren't starving. They've had their fill of kisses. No use talking! Rip their bellies open—something a bit tastier than porridge and offal inside 'em.

OLD MAN. Lock up your homes and workshops, brothers, abandon your wives, mothers, mistresses, get yourselves out in the street and wait. The hour is nigh. The reign of the Antichrist has begun. Don't serve in the army, don't pay taxes, don't sign up, don't get qualified—all that is the mark of the Antichrist. Come on out, all of you, and we'll be as one body. In unity lies our salvation.

VOICES. Away with that buffoon! Into a sack with him! Better put Nero in a sack! Long time he's been asking for it. We want bread! We want bread! Defeat in Britain, disaster in Armenia, secession in Syria. And he never leaves off singing. The stars threaten calamity. An avenger has appeared in Gaul. Vindex, that's what he's called. Long live Vindex! The legions are advancing on Rome. The Gaulish cock will crow the dawn of liberation.

WOMEN. How long will we be standing in lines, how long will we be feeding on oats? Losers and layabouts—griping on the sly, that's all you're good for. Not a man among you. Just a lot of old women. Worse than women. See that ship for Alexandria with grain on board? What are you just staring at it for? Grab hold of the grain-sacks and drag 'em away! Good-for-nothings. Just you try getting into bed with us—we'll give you a taste of the broom.

VOICES. What's the point of gaping, lads? That there boat! Break her up!

> They rush toward the ship.

POLICEMAN. Citizens, keep calm, no rash behavior, you will receive everything in due time.

VOICES. Due time? And when may that be? In four years—that's what we've been told. By that time we'll all have croaked. On board, get on board!

Scuffling with sailors on the ship's deck.

WOMAN. Romans, no holding back. Let him have it! Let him have it!

VOICES. Drag those sacks off! Throw them down here. What's this? Sand!

SHIPOWNER. Scum, sons-of-bitches, citizens, comrades. Grain's the last thing you'll find there—just sand for the circus arena. The Emperor ordered it from Alexandria.

VOICES. Into the water with the Egyptian. Down with Nero! Into the cesspit with him, into the cesspit. Long live Vindex! Kill the Christians and save Rome! Down with the arsonist! Down with the murderer!

A scream.

ACT III
1st Tableau

The fire at the hotel is dying down. PAVEL is on the roof. He is surrounded by policemen.

PAVEL. Tidings of great joy! Tidings of great joy!

He is arrested and escorted from the roof. Below, MARIE and FRIEDRICH approach the police officer in command.

MARIE. Colonel, this is a complete misunderstanding. It's true, my husband is Russian, but he isn't mixed up in any kind of politics. You can check on that. He's just a sick man. He may be insane. I can put down bail for him right now, whatever sum you name.

COLONEL. Impossible.

MARIE. I'm only asking you to send him to the clinic for an examination. I'm not asking for his release. I understand.

But you too should understand that a person of sound
mind wouldn't be behaving in the way Mr. Lukin is.

COLONEL. Impossible.

MARIE. Friedrich! (*FRIEDRICH gets out his wallet.*) Colonel,
do take this, please. I beg of you. You say: Impossible. But
it's just a formality. Maybe it isn't your direct responsibil-
ity, but it cannot be impossible.

PAVEL is escorted from the hotel.

Just look at him. He's obviously not in his right mind. As a
policeman and as a colonel, you should also be a psycholo-
gist—and a perceptive one. Have him put in a clinic, and
then you can have a good look at him. Take the money. This
should be enough. And please don't refuse me the kindness
of keeping me informed—I mean you, you personally—about
how the situation is developing. I'm putting up at No. 17. Is it
all right? I'll be waiting to hear from you.

COLONEL. It is all right. It looks as if you may be right.
You've got common sense.

MARIE. Do you find that surprising?

COLONEL. All the best.

MARIE. Good-bye.

PAVEL is led away.

MARIE. Friedrich. I'm going to faint. Hold me. What are we
to do?

FRIEDRICH. Good thing we have a delay. Gives us time to
think.

MARIANNA comes toward them.

MARIANNA. Our people will snatch him.

MARIE. And who may they be?

MARIANNA. Mr. Lukin's friends.

MARIE (*to FRIEDRICH*). Do you know her?

FRIEDRICH. I've got an idea who she is.

MARIE. Apparently you have an interest in the fate of Pavel
Andreyevich?

MARIANNA. I do.

MARIE. And it would seem that you don't have any kind of
profession or occupation?

MARIANNA. Profession?

MARIE. I didn't mean to offend you. I just wanted to know. Perhaps you love Pavel Andreyevich? (*MARIANNA is silent.*) Hmm, that's exactly what I thought. You know, Friedrich, this is starting to resemble one of those cheap novels.

MARIANNA. If things were only the way you say they are.

MARIE. You silly girl! I'm beginning to like you. Let's go. Tell us what happens in the next chapter, the one about the abduction.

Exeunt.

2ⁿᵈ Tableau

A hallway in the palace. Nero enters hurriedly with SPORUS, ACTEA, WET-NURSE, PHAON and retinue. Things done up in packages are carried in.

NERO. Now that was a rush! But it looks as if I'm on time. All the same, I won't be going to the Senate today. Take them a letter, convey my apologies, tell them I've got quinsy. You know, I really do feel a tickling in my throat. And it's better not to do things in a hurry. I'm not a child, I'm not in the least afraid of them.

COURTIER. They've started calling you not Nero but Enobarbus.

NERO. An odd bunch! Doesn't it come to the same thing, Emperor Nero or Emperor Enobarbus—isn't it the same me? Excellent, I'm no longer Nero—from this moment I'll be signing myself Enobarbus. Why offend my great-grandfather?

COURTIER. To insult you—that was their intention.

NERO. But I don't take it as an insult, so they are the losers. I won't forget it, though. Generally speaking, there's nothing to be upset about. The astrologers have told me that, whatever may happen, I am assured of an eastern kingdom. I'm hesitating between Parthia and Jerusalem. They warned me against the age seventy-three. You hear? I am guaranteed another forty-one years of life—and that means as sovereign. Aha! All plans will have time to be realized. Yes, the universe is the prop of genius. Well, how about a bite of something? Don't hang your head, Sporus, we'll live to see another day. No one would dream of doubting it. I am completely calm. No sooner had I entered the city than I saw a statue of a Roman dragging a Gaul along by the hair. Clearly an omen. Oh yes, and today we'll be inaugurating the new water organ. See that it's in working order. First we'll listen to it among ourselves, then tomorrow or on Tuesday we'll summon guests. So where's dinner? Oh, has everything been brought in? They're sure to have forgotten something. We had to get things ready in such a hurry. Are the garlands here? Excellent. The potions, the case for the lyre. Say what you like, all this is very unpleasant.

SPORUS. Calm down. Your thoughts are jumping from one thing to another.

NERO. That's natural—there are too many things to be thought of all at the same time.

COURIER. A message. (*Hands NERO a letter.*)

NERO (*having skimmed the letter*). A retreat? Because of that? Damnation!

WET NURSE. Now calm down, sonny-boy, it often happens. There have been greater heroes than you, and even they knew defeat, even they came crashing down like felled oak trees. The sun will come out again. Be patient. Misfortune can happen to anyone.

NERO. To anyone? No. The misfortunes of Nero, just like his greatness, are reserved for him alone. But they shall know my anger! Invite the whole Senate to supper *in corpore* and poison the lot at one go. Locusta knows how to do that. Let her be provided with the means to obtain the ingredients. Let Rome be set on fire in all four corners. Let wild beasts prowl the streets. Then these nincompoops will take to their heels. Get him! Tear him apart! Slaughter every Gaul in the city. Every one of them—women, old folk, babies! Slaughter them all! What's this? Ah, a bite to eat . . . Good, set it down here. Essentially, nothing of real importance has happened. Local uprisings, minor defeats are unavoidable in such a vast state. Excuse me, gentlemen, for eating in your presence. I am a man of the road. I may be excused. (*Soft music.*) The organ? Who turned it on without my permission? But it's entirely appropriate. What fullness and tenderness sound gains from distance! They say the movement of the planets generates music—it is called the music of the spheres. This is probably just what that is like. Do you like it, Sporus? Just from a distance. Like the blessing of demons.

Enter COURIER.

COURIER. From the Senate.

NERO reads the document through, leaps to his feet, knocking over table and dishes, throws document down.

COURTIER (*having picked it up, reads it*). As the enemy of the people . . . To be flayed alive.

NERO. Well, what are you standing there for? Don't unwrap things. We're going to Parthia, to Ostia. The ship is ready. The wind is favorable. What? Who's with me? What did you say? "Can it really be so difficult to die?" You were the one who said that, you bastard! (*He punches one of the courtiers.*) But why should I run away? All I have to do is to go out on the square, give a speech, shed a few tears, make a show of repentance, make a few promises, and they'll be at my feet again. Am I devoid of talent? The people love me, and they do have a feeling for art. What's that? They won't let me approach? They'll tear me apart? Then kill me. Specillius, you are a gladiator, you know how to use a weapon, I've always been good to you. Here is a sword. What? Does this mean I have neither friends nor enemies? I forgot to bring the poison from Naples. Sporus, let's drown ourselves in the Tiber together. We'll tie ourselves to one another and drown. You did love me. What's that? Why is the organ playing?

PHAON. Emperor, hide in my villa. Wait out the bad weather. But don't dawdle. Every second is numbered.

NERO. Yes, yes. Why hadn't I thought of that! You're a friend. I see that. I promote you to the rank of general. Where are the horses, then? Quick! Quick!

COURTIER. Change your shoes. You've got slippers on. They'll fall off while you're riding.

NERO. What are slippers when thrones, altars, gods and stars are falling?

Exeunt.

The organ continues to play.

3rd **Tableau**

The yard of an insane asylum. Everything is
symmetrical and clean. Groups of patients are
sitting, standing and walking about. PAVEL sits
motionless among them. From the white
outbuilding come sounds of a harmonium.
Gounod's "Ave Maria."

1ST MADMAN (*standing on a barrel*). Gentlemen, this sheet of
paper contains the essence of many years—of an entire
lifetime, many generations. The secret of immortality and
of happiness. It is called "Tidings of Great Joy." You are
requested not to confuse this name with "Gospel," which
can also be translated "Tidings of Great Joy." I have decided to be the benefactor of humanity and make this treasure available to all free of charge. Get in line, gentlemen,
for "Tidings of Great Joy."

2ND MADMAN. There haven't been any gentlemen for some
time now, and the same goes for the Lord above. What does
"Lord" mean? A combination of letters. You have to know
how to make sense of them, the same way we make sense
of LSPO. It can be interpreted in any way you like. Everyone has his own interpretation, because the word has no
meaning in itself and doesn't express any concept. Same
with "Lord." A mechanical combination of letters. So there
is no Lord above. And there is no God. Where is He? Here
I am, saying there's no God—and never a word from on
high. Why doesn't He say anything? Because He doesn't
exist.

OLD WOMAN. Idiot, that's what you are, an idiot. "Why
doesn't He say anything?" Because He doesn't fancy listen-
ing to you.

2ND MADMAN. Unconvincing. Unprovable.

3rd MADMAN hits 2nd MADMAN over the head with
a watering can.

2nd MADMAN. Thoroughly uncivilized behavior.

3RD MADMAN. But convincing.

SUPERVISOR. Gentlemen. Keep calm. No excesses.

GIRL (*going up to PAVEL*). I know who you are. But don't be
afraid, I won't give you away. I understand that you are not

the man they take you for. But you aren't an impostor, though everyone considers you to be a deceiver. You are the man. It is as it was foretold. All the tokens coincide. And I did attend your funeral, which was nothing but a confidence trick. They buried someone else, or a puppet, or no one at all. When you were lying on the ground, your eyes were wide-open, and so godlike did you appear that nobody dared come close. Then you arose and went your way. He knew. And they too knew, those Jewesses of yours. They knew they were adorning an empty grave with flowers. Secretly, covertly, stealthily the whole world has been awaiting your coming. And you have come. You have come for the third time. And many more times will you be coming. You have the mark upon you. The faithful know it. Below your left nipple. I know.

PAVEL. So who am I in your opinion?

GIRL. What do you mean, who? You—you are Nero.

PAVEL. Nero? The Roman emperor?

GIRL. Of course. From me you don't have to hide. With my own eyes I have seen you. (*Sits down beside him.*)

MARIANNA, eccentrically costumed, comes walking across the stage from the other side.

MARIANNA. Mr. Lukin. Don't be surprised. Be quiet and listen.

PAVEL. But who can you be?

MARIANNA. You will remember. After all, your memory is unharmed. You are here for your salvation.

PAVEL. Marianna?

MARIANNA. Of course. But speak softly.

PAVEL. What are you doing here? Are you ill?

MARIANNA. No more than you are. Don't ask questions. Friends are keeping vigil and waiting for you. Do not resist.

PAVEL. How is Marie? How is Friedrich?

MARIANNA. Everything will become clear to you. Give me your hand. Let's make a run for it, as if we were playing "catch." Nobody will be surprised. The guard has been bribed. There's a car waiting round the corner. You are greatly loved.

PAVEL. Marie? Friedrich?

MARIANNA. Later, later. Let's run for it.

Taking hands they run off and are lost to view. The
harmonium continues to play.

4ᵗʰ Tableau

A road near Rome. A sentry box. Night, a
thunderstorm. NERO and three companions are on
horseback. NERO is barefoot. His face is covered.

NERO. Quiet. Someone is coming. I'm sure to be recognized.

Comes to a halt in the darkness.

1ˢᵀ PASSERBY. I think I heard someone on horseback.
2ᴺᴰ PASSERBY. Probably in pursuit of Nero. They're chasing
him from every direction.
1ˢᵀ PASSERBY. Could he have fled?
2ᴺᴰ PASSERBY. So they say. No one knows for sure.
1ˢᵀ PASSERBY. An odd story.
2ᴺᴰ PASSERBY. Yes, very. And the weather is a bit odd, too.
A dry storm, but without heat.
1ˢᵀ PASSERBY. If Nero is caught, they'll flay him alive. Such
is the law. It's never been put into practice, though.
2ᴺᴰ PASSERBY. Have they sworn allegiance to Galba yet?
1ˢᵀ PASSERBY. Not yet. They'll be taking the oath this evening.
2ᴺᴰ PASSERBY. Let's move on, then. There's nobody on
horseback. You simply misheard.

They move on.

1ˢᵀ PASSERBY. Probably I did.
NERO. They've gone! (*He stumbles over a corpse.*) What's this?
A corpse?
COMPANION. There's a plague in the city. People just drop
dead.

A flash of lightning. The cloth over NERO's face is
blown aside by the wind. The soldier at the sentry
box comes to attention.

NERO. He recognized me and saluted! Loyalty, betrayal,
honor, dishonor, people, gods, fate, myself—in a single mo-

ment I begin to understand everything, as if I were new to this life.

COMPANION. Hurry, let's hurry. It'll be dawn before long.

5th Tableau

The same road near Rome. Ruins. An automobile
pulls up. MARIE and FRIEDRICH.

MARIE. Stop.

FRIEDRICH. You want to wait for them?

MARIE. But what are we going to do?

FRIEDRICH. Now the situation isn't that critical. Looks like his escape will be a success. You'll cross the border, and you'll live the life you did before.

MARIE. No, that's all over. Don't you feel that yourself, Friedrich? We have slithered down an enormous mounting. It's a landslide.

FRIEDRICH. But essentially nothing has happened.

MARIE. Nothing could have happened where nothing was. Pavel's monstrous confidence that anything can be attained with money has collapsed.

FRIEDRICH. He never said such a thing.

MARIE. But that's how he acted. You can't be a benefactor of humanity without seeing people as they are. But he didn't see either me or you or anyone else. To him we are phantoms, numbers, grains of sand. Oh, how I hate that word: humanity.

FRIEDRICH. You hate Pavel, too?

MARIE. I hate him, he knows that. Nobody can live when he owes his life to somebody else. Pavel isn't God.

FRIEDRICH. Why are you telling me all this?

MARIE. You are clever: what I am saying does indeed have a goal. Friedrich, for once in your life, do something as if you had a will of your own: let events roll into the abyss without us.

FRIEDRICH. What do you mean?

MARIE. Let's turn the wheel. It doesn't matter where to, but in some other direction.

FRIEDRICH. Abandon Pavel?

MARIE. But didn't he abandon us?

FRIEDRICH. No, no.

MARIE. He has perished anyway. He died. Let us live.

FRIEDRICH. How?

MARIE. Passion and danger.

FRIEDRICH. It's a crime.

MARIE. Why should we worry what it's called? Do the letters of the alphabet frighten you?

FRIEDRICH. I don't want to be a betrayer.

MARIE. But aren't you afraid of being the betrayer of your own life? Friedrich, you do love me, don't you?

FRIEDRICH. I do. I've loved you from the moment we met. My life is at your disposal—but I will not betray Pavel.

MARIE. Betrayal will fall on me, on me alone.

FRIEDRICH. But I refuse to be a part of it, to be an instrument of it.

MARIE. You refuse?

FRIEDRICH. Yes.

MARIE. It doesn't matter. I have a fever, a natural one—just feel my pulse. Forget this conversation—go and see if the others are coming.

> FRIEDRICH walks away. MARIE takes out a
> revolver. She shoots FRIEDRICH, then herself. The
> revolver drops from her hand, firing a third shot.

MARIE (*as she falls*). At last I am alive! (*Dies.*)

FRIEDRICH (*as he falls*). How silly, Marie. (*Dies.*)

> Another automobile pulls up.

PAVEL. What is this? Dead bodies? Can there be a plague in the city? Who's this—Marie? Friedrich? They've both been killed? Why didn't you leave me in the asylum?

MARIANNA. You'll find out later. Let's go, let's go.

PAVEL. Everything has come to an end.

MARIANNA. Nothing has come to an end. From this moment everything is beginning for you. Let's go!

> They drive off.

6th Tableau

> Dawn. A garden at Phaon's house. A narrow gap in
> the wall, through which two people crawl; they then
> pull NERO through with an effort. PHAON, ACTEA

and two wet nurses come out of the house. SPORUS
has rapidly crawled through in NERO's wake. The
women immediately prostrate themselves at
NERO's bare feet.

PHAON. Welcome, Emperor. Forgive me your uncomfortable entrance.
NERO. It reminded me of a dream I once had. I was making
my way through an extremely narrow corridor, and I knew
that beyond it lay something unknown. It was horrible, and
ever since then narrow passageways have scared me.
PHAON. Beyond this corridor lies salvation, or at least a
chance to take a rest, if only briefly.
NERO. I'm terribly thirsty.
PHAON. I'll bring you something right away. Bear in mind
that this is an abandoned house, I haven't lived here for
ages—so you won't find any creature comforts. I thought
the place's abandoned state guaranteed greater security.
I'll go look for some bread and water.
NERO. Not worth it. I'm not hungry, and there's probably
still some water over there, in that hollow under the water
pipe.

One of the women goes quickly, and with some
difficulty scoops a handful of water, which she
offers to NERO. He drinks.

NERO. Marvelous. I've never drunk anything so tasty. Deprivations reveal new delights. How strange that is! But the
last stretch of the way here was dreadful. Over a field of
stubble. I found myself to be completely incapable of going
anywhere on foot. Who would ever have dreamed that such
a skill would come in handy? A funny picture we must
have presented when you spread a cloak for me and I took
three steps, came to a halt and you spread another cloak,
three more steps, another halt—and so on. Good thing it
was only about a quarter of a mile. What's the matter,
Phaon? You're turning away? You're crying? Am I really
that pathetic?
PHAON. That's not why I'm crying, Emperor.
NERO. Why are you, then? (*PHAON is silent.*) Tell me, am I
completely out of danger?
PHAON. For the time being.

NERO. Find me a safer refuge then.

PHAON. When they were building this house, they got sand from close by. Then the pit was abandoned, as everything here was. There are deep caverns there. In a rush they're unlikely to be searched.

NERO. A sandpit? No, no . . . sand can fall in on you. Why should I bury myself alive? Is there no escaping destruction? (*PHAON is silent.*) You're an honest man, Phaon, but honesty is merciless. Seeing that I am condemned, you could at least make these moments more tranquil for me. But there must be some chance, some happy chance. All this story has been nothing but misfortune for me—but that can always be averted by some happy chance. Can't it? You don't think so? All the same; inevitable chance is neither lawful nor equitable by virtue of its inevitability. Oh, if only this cup would pass from me!

> The women gradually break into a wail,
> which—now weaker, now stronger—continues
> uninterrupted.

NERO. Very well then! Let them heat water for the cleansing rite, let my new year's robes be brought to me. Icelus did promise, didn't he?

PHAON. Yes, Icelus did promise to release the body for burial.

NERO. Body? Me—a body already? Hand me the daggers; this one seems a bit sharper. But it isn't time yet, is it? You will tell me, honest Phaon, when it's time. O Sporus, if you only knew the misery that overwhelms me. Misery and longing . . . The naked man is what I've always been in search of, and that's why I've always loved catastrophic events, thinking that it's then man's simplest feelings— unalloyed, uncontrolled—appear. And what comes of that? These feelings are no different from an animal's—dog, cat, rabbit, hen, sparrow, lion if you like. That's nothing to be proud of. Nero is the same as everyone else. But however that may be, I did want to make everyone happy and I did have a sincere love of art—such was my devotion to art that with me dies . . . (*shudders*) that with my passing the world is deprived of a true artist. What, Phaon, you're giving me a signal already?

PHAON. I hear the sound of hooves.

NERO. You could have misheard.
PHAON. No.
NERO. Weep louder. It gives me strength. Farewell, Phaon, and you, and you—farewell. Farewell, my dearest Sporus—what will became of you without me? Epaphroditus gives me this dagger, the sharpest one, now I take it in my hand, I cover my head with my cloak. Now take the hand with the dagger in it . . . here, where the heart beats . . . take it, take it, don't be afraid, firmly. And . . . that's right.

Falls.

Enter CENTURION.

CENTURION. Emperor, you are wounded! (*Covers him with his cloak.*)
NERO. There's loyalty for you. (*Dies. The sun rises.*)

7ᵗʰ Tableau

Switzerland. A large, bright room with a garden terrace. Sun. Enter PAVEL and DOCTOR.

PAVEL. I'm not dead, then?
DOCTOR. What do you mean?
PAVEL. Well, am I alive?
DOCTOR. Of course. What a question.
PAVEL. I'm not in the next world?
DOCTOR. No, you're in Switzerland.
PAVEL. This isn't a hospital, it's not a lunatic asylum?
DOCTOR. No, it's a country house, and you'll be living here until you recover.
PAVEL. But you are a doctor?
DOCTOR. I am a doctor, but that's simply a coincidence. I happen to be the owner of this house, which a relative is renting for you; it's as simple as that. Your health has improved considerably.
PAVEL. I may be healthy, but it's as if I'm in a dream—there's something I don't remember, something I don't know.
DOCTOR. But you remember that your wife shot your friend and then committed suicide?

PAVEL. I remember perfectly. Aren't these leading questions?

DOCTOR. And you know that you've lost all your money?

PAVEL. I know, though I don't remember who informed me of it.

DOCTOR. Now you have to start life again.

PAVEL. Life?

DOCTOR. Of course. And on completely different principles. Let humanity take care of itself; you are a man and you must take care of that man. And stop thinking of yourself as a benefactor. You are like a child now, without strength, without means, but now you understand what there is no strength in, what cannot serve as means. You know where the false path is—and that in itself is an achievement.

PAVEL. So you are simply the owner of this country house, no more than that.

DOCTOR. Yes. What I am telling you is what you would hear from any man who had not been infected by an abstract dream.

PAVEL. Yes, Marianna was telling me something along those lines. She's a kind girl. Where is she, by the way? If I'm not mistaken, it was she who brought me here.

DOCTOR. It was, but she went away as soon as she saw another person, one with whom you will be learning to live again. You are still weak. One person is enough for you.

PAVEL. Who can it be? Is he the mysterious relative who is renting this house for me?

DOCTOR. Yes.

PAVEL. Some distant relative on my father's side? I can't think of anybody somehow.

DOCTOR. No, on the contrary, this person was very close to your late father—and is close to you.

PAVEL. Who is he?

DOCTOR. Your brother.

PAVEL. My brother! But he's only a boy.

DOCTOR. He's ten years younger than you are, but he is already twenty-two. Don't forget you are almost thirty-three.

PAVEL. He will be living with me? He is coming here?

DOCTOR. He's here already, and he will be living with you. He'll be here in a moment.

PAVEL. Doctor, even if you are no more than just a landlord, don't leave me alone! For the first moment, just the first moment.

DOCTOR. It's better that you meet without witnesses.

PAVEL. But not right now. I'm not prepared. Father was unfair to him in his will. I hardly know him, he was such a handsome boy that I cannot . . .

DOCTOR. Don't worry. He doesn't consider himself to have been unjustly treated at all; he's not rich, but he's quite well off; for the present and for a long time to come, his sole concern will be to help you right what you did wrong. Whether or not he's handsome you can judge for yourself—here he is, walking through the garden.

PAVEL. What? Already? It's him? Doctor, I've probably got a fever. If I were a believer, I would think that an angel was coming across the lawn. Doctor, I must be delirious. I think he looks like me.

DOCTOR. What's surprising about that? You are brothers.

PAVEL. Doctor, don't go.

DOCTOR. It's time I did.

PAVEL. At least tell me what his name is.

DOCTOR. Fyodor Andreyevich. I thought you knew. (*Exit.*)

PAVEL. Doctor! He's gone . . . (*He takes a long look out of the window. Eventually he steps quickly onto the terrace.*)

PAVEL'S VOICE. Fedya!

8ᵗʰ Tableau

Nero's porphyry crypt. Garden on a hill. Altar.
Moon. Hanging garlands. Sad music. ACTEA, the
two wet nurses and several women prepare to
leave.

1ˢᵀ WET NURSE. His memory will not fade.

2ᴺᴰ WET NURSE. May the gloom of the infernal regions not be burdensome to him. How godlike his face was, with those white wide-open eyes. Even the soldiers drew back, as if they were stepping on holy, plague-stricken soil. I still can't believe he's dead. Wasn't it you who washed the body, who anointed it, who wrapped the shroud about it? Demons are powerful, they can take any shape. He was possessed by demons. By the demon Ailus. Good fortune was his; he linked his fate with the little doll Tyukhe, and he lost her. She fell in the water while he was fishing, and there was no finding her.

Enter GIRL.

GIRL. Oh I'm late. The emperor has already been buried. So
I won't see him again? (*Weeps.*)
WOMAN. But where did you see him? You're not from these
parts. You've got a Greek accent. And you're not one of the
court maidservants either. Who are you? Where are you
from? What's your name?
GIRL. I'm from Corinth and my name is Tyukhe. I saw the
emperor only once in my life, but I remembered him forever. After my parents died, I used to sell flowers and to
dance when there were guests to entertain. One day I noticed that the streets were terribly crowded; I never
thought Corinth had so many people, as if they'd all been
herded together from the five cities. Everyone was making
for the same place. The emperor was passing through.
What luxury there was, what glitter! But I didn't see any of
that. My eyes were fixed on the emperor alone. He was
robed in silver, seemed absent and thoughtful, and on his
head was a garland of gold. But it was hard to make out the
gold against the gold of his hair, and you didn't know
where the radiance was coming from—the garland or his
hair. I stood on tiptoe, not noticing the tears rolling down
my cheeks. The emperor suddenly fixes his eyes on me
alone in the whole crowd and says: "Little girl, what are
you crying for? Do you have some sorrow, some pain? Tell
me: I can do anything, I am Nero."—"I'm crying because I
see you, divine one."—"What's your name?"—"Tyukhe."—
"Tyukhe? You have a lucky name, and rarely have I come
across such a pretty girl."—And then he went his way. I can
never forget this. From that time on, if I get sad, or someone offends me, if some little misfortune comes my way, I
remember that I have a lucky name, and that there is an
emperor who has rarely come across such a pretty girl as
me. And then I feel such a warmth, such a calm, my heart
begins to sing, my hands go flying up in the air, people I
need turn up right in front of me, my wrongs are forgotten,
and I feel myself to be under the protection of the divine
demon Nero. Who he is—man or deity—I do not know, but
this I do know: if I lay dead and he summoned me, I would
arise and go to him. I hoarded money to come here and get
another look at him—but now I hear that he's no more, that
he has died. You seem to be good women, and your cheeks

are wet with tears—so it must be true. Perhaps it's some kind of trickery, and the emperor is still alive? To me you can tell the truth, I won't give you away. How could Nero die, whose very name to me sounds like tidings of great joy?

WOMAN. Tyukhe! Tyukhe! She has been found, she is not lost, they got her out of the water somehow, she has come back to Nero, his little girl, the one who watches over him, Tyukhe. Thrice blessed art thou, newcomer, herald of life!

The End.

July 8, 1929

Prose

"High Art"

for Nikolai Gumilev

I USED TO KNOW KONSTANTIN PETROVICH, OR KOSTYA, SHCHETIN-kin as far back as my spell in a provincial town, when he was a schoolboy. Not that I knew him particularly well, but the house of the Shchetinkin family bordered the yard and straggling orchard of my auntie's house, and my little boy and girl cousins enjoyed the company of their neighbors' lively and mischievous son. Of course, there was no lack of squabbles, but they would be settled either by the yardkeeper's wife and maid of all work Mavra or by the coachman Luka—only in exceptional cases would they get as far as auntie. She, with her frivolous, unconcerned nature and gentle permissiveness would soon smooth over rough patches that, with other parents, would inevitably have led to family dissension. Most likely he was neither a bad boy nor a good one; high-spirited he was, and by no means stupid, a bristle-haired, snub-nosed gingerhead. I used to spend only the summer in our town, so I always saw Kostya Shchetinkin covered in freckles, tanned, dressed in a dirty, out-at-elbow jacket.

It wasn't long before auntie moved to Moscow. Since the children were all growing up, some thought had to be given to their further education. I, possessing in her my only link with the provinces, began to forget our little town, rarely calling gingerheaded Kostya to mind.

In this way eight years passed, and summers in the warm little house on the Volga receded into a cherished distance, seeming almost like childhood. The uneasy years of Russia's latest "crisis" went by; everyone began to wake up from their drowse only to roll over and start snuffling once more. Many faces had disappeared from the scene, while yet others came into sight; I too had changed with the times—when a chance mention of Shchetinkin's name gave me a start and made me recall many things from the past.

195

The cherished, irrecoverable past—what a warmth it breathed. Auntie, who by now had passed away, and the long narrow orchard came to mind—together with much else in which Kostya played no part but with which he was somehow linked. And what particularly interested me was that I was hearing things about Kostya in a place where I would least have expected to. I remember that Shchetinkin's name came up—what's more, as that of a very promising young poet—at the home of the writer Adventov. Opinions were hotly divided, which almost always serves to demonstrate something's significance. Upon inquiry, I learned that this poet of promise was exactly the same young fellow I had caught red-handed several times stealing unripe apples in auntie's orchard. All the more flattering for me to see what he had become. When I learned one day at this very house, of which I was at that time an assiduous frequenter, that young Shchetinkin was among those present, I gazed with reinforced curiosity at this gingerhead, bristlehaired as ever, with the gleaming row of large teeth he would frequently display in an embarrassed smile. I recognized him immediately, and when he introduced himself, extending a small hand, red as a goose's foot, I began chatting with him as with an old acquaintance. Losing his awkwardness, he turned out to be, as in the old days, lively, energetic and obviously no fool. Well-wishers with one voice praised his talent as volatile, piquant and remarkable in its originality, a judgment confirmed, as far as it could be, by the verse he read on this occasion. It was said that he also occupied himself with a like-spirited prose: sprightly, whimsical, diverting, never the least bit dull—no mean feat, given regulation Russian tedium, with its dutiful mastication of Chekhovian neurasthenia. Such prose, if it does take wing, does so in a Juvenalian vein not always marked either by good judgment or good sense. In short, I willingly joined a company of cautious, not unduly skeptical bystanders not too young to dismiss the visibly developing talent of Konstantin Petrovich. We were not so moribund as to deliver ourselves of the scornful arrogance of wilting snobs, so often accompanied by general-like grunts and "barked" commands.

Later, when Shchetinkin began dropping by, I found him to have an absorbing character. He seemed to me to represent a new type of human being, one that—for good or ill—is to be met with increasing frequency. Not in the least a dreamer, but not an obtuse positivist either, he did not seem preoccupied with general questions, although he did, at the same time, have ready answers—always precise and definite, if sometimes self-contradictory—to all the problems of life, be they abstract or concrete. Though extremely hardworking and conscientious, he had buoyancy and an insatiable relish for life. His attitude to the world was levelheaded and could undoubtedly have brought down on his head accusations of lack of principle—an attitude not pardoned him by persons of widely divergent views. Such practicality in his perception of the world, if not in the conduct of his own affairs, such firmness, such ability to restrict his concerns to the demands of reality (plus a certain measured heartlessness compounded with gentleness and buoyancy) seemed to me of great portent. I would have been prepared to consider Shchetinkin a strong individual, had not the subsequent development of his history cruelly refuted such a definition. However, as will be evident to the reader from the following narrative, blame is to be laid not so much on Kostya's weakness as on the influence of a personage of utterly opposed moods and aspirations—and one who was closely connected with Shchetinkin.

A fair amount of time passed, and by the decree of the fates I somehow lost track of Shchetinkin, having troubles of my own to deal with and a certain disposition inclining me to work in solitude. If I did venture forth, it was to visit a sick friend confined to a military hospital. Of an evening I would climb the stairs from my own quarters to the apartment of an amiable family whose relaxed talk and genuine affection for me greatly relieved my difficult moments. From my "beautiful remoteness" I did not cease to follow my new acquaintance's literary strides; I was pleased to see that, though not equipped with seven-league boots, he strode boldly and confidently along his own path. When my spiritual turmoil had passed and I broke my self-imposed seclusion, beginning to go out again, I learned that Shchetinkin had married. Whom it was he had married nobody could explain precisely, his wife not coming from our immediate circle. She was called Zoya Nikolayevna—which was also less than informative. The news, of course, I met with complete indifference, thinking the young man probably knew what he was about, also confident that he was sensible and practical enough. So he had married—wasn't it all the same to me? No doubt that was how it had to be.

Winter that year (1907—1908) came suddenly: fierce frosts began in November, setting in for two months without the usual Petersburg thaws. One such evening I took the risk of abandoning my cell. Steam came in clouds from horses as well as from men muffled in fur coats; smoke floated up from every chimney and spread in a blue haze against the un-clouded moon, bonfires burned in iron braziers; everything indoors seemed comfortable and cozy, and over the Neva snow, sky and the Admiralty needle hymned by Pushkin gleamed azure; sledges creaked and more than one "beaver collar was silvered with frostdust." I set out in the direction of a distant theater for the premier of a play by an acquain-tance of mine whose work was pronounced perfection in our circle, while still found to be daring and controversial by the public at large. I wasn't particularly eager to go, having yet to regain my old sociable habits, but I took a certain pleasure in the expectation of seeing, if only from a distance, the soci-ety friends I had been missing.

In the lobby, before I had even managed to take off my overcoat, I ran into a number of friends; on the way to my seat, I was stopped by none other than Konstantin Petrovich himself. He naturally introduced me to his spouse, who turned out to be a comely lady—tall, lissome, with fine, some-what severe features, a large mouth and blond locks. She was smartly, even a little extravagantly dressed, and Shchetinkin too had a dandified air. Addressing me, she declared that al-though we were not acquainted, she knew me well. This I thought mere conventional politeness, unfitted to so extrava-gant a personage. But when she informed me of her maiden name, I realized that this was not only true, but that if she did indeed know me, I knew her, too: in the past we had met quite often.

Zoya Nikolayevna Gorbunova was one of the six daughters of our former vice-governor, and had once dazzled the whole town with her wit, her coquetry, the freedom of her behavior.

With money, social standing and ambition, it is not difficult in the provinces to create such a "dazzling" reputation for oneself: a random acquaintance with contemporary litera-ture in four languages, childish pranks—quite harmless, if frequently in poor taste—at the expense of the peaceful bur-ghers. A certain atavistic *Georgesandisme*, a combination of "tomboy" and "eccentric English miss," a touch of the blue-stocking and a great deal of the regimental *grande dame*—all this produced a female centaur in the latest style, one who was difficult to endure. Miss Gorbunova, it must be granted, did have a decent education and a marvelous "gift of tongues," which is to say, she had a sound knowledge of foreign languages and made use of her own with a certain bravado. All this glitter, needless to say, was of a rather second-rate variety, but amidst the tedium of provincial existence it was diverting in small doses, if not truly out of the ordinary. Whatever the occupation—poetry, singing, sport, the stage or decorating porcelain—Zoya Nikolayevna threw herself into it with equal fervor, without, however, quite managing to "find herself."

It had been my conviction—dare I confess?—that her main vocation was to get herself a husband; but I would never have dreamed that her choice would fall on Kostya Shchetin-kin—in her eyes, surely, an utterly insignificant person. All this was on my mind during the play, which turned out to be so tedious that I was annoyed both with the public for their enthusiasm and with the author himself, who had provided no grounds for indignation at an audience's failure to comprehend. Observing the Shchetinkins, seated not far from me, I noted in the figure, face and manner of Zoya Nikolay-evna something that brought to mind a Polish woman, or rather a Russian woman putting on Polish airs. I had no opportunity of speaking with the young couple during the intervals, and we contented ourselves with exchanging smiles of greeting as we passed. Only at the end, as the audience was dispersing, did Zoya Nikolayevna refuse to let me go until I had pledged to pay them a visit in the near future. It turned out that I had not been completely correct in my characterization of the new literary lady. Having married, she had not abandoned her dreams. Discharging the other arts, she now confined herself to poetry, obsessed with her plans for future literary productions. On all sides I heard praise of her beauty, an intelligence excelling that of her sex, of her talent, and—this was the main thing—of her "power to infect." It was said that she had such a stock of enthusiasm that it sufficed for those around her, who took fire like dry rubbish from a match. All her theorizing, all her lucubrations and exultations were focused on the concept of "high art." This I found somewhat difficult to coordinate with the talent of her husband, which seemed to be taking a path in the opposite direction. At first he had perhaps been a little overshadowed, yielding his place to Zoya Nikolayevna's discourses. I say "discourses" because nobody ever heard her literary compositions—accepting them, as it were, on credit. Well, who hasn't made a mistake! Perhaps I had been wrong to write her off as no more than a vice-gubernatorial young miss playing the decadent when she really was the "firebird" we had all been waiting for.

This was a time when mysterious poetesses had yet to come into vogue—before there was such an abundance of literary lionesses. If Unknown Ladies, both Spanish and Rumanian, did make an appearance, it was only for the sake of publicity, or for some completely different purpose. Thus it was that Zoya became the preoccupation of all who were not too indolent and who had sufficient leisure to meddle in the affairs of others. But I, too, taking my example from these charming folk, was determined to resolve the puzzle for myself, to present my own solution of the incompatible compatibility of "high-arty" Mme. Shchetinkina and down-to-earth Kostya.

Having breached my solitude with a visit to the theater, I could hardly beat a retreat. I no longer had a reasonable excuse for postponing my visit to Vasilevsky Island, where the young Shchetinkins had settled. One twilight evening, having time on my hands, I buried my nose in my collar and set off from my own suburb, the Tavricheskaya Embankment, for another one. The young couple had established themselves most satisfactorily: their quarters were uncramped, not too high up, and far from impoverished, being equipped with servants, electricity, an elevator and other creature comforts. Glancing at the art nouveau decor of the lobby, at the maidservant in matching style, at the posies of violets adorning the lobby, I had the thought that practical Kostya had not been imprudent, and that if the vice-governor's daughter had brought such well-being in her train, one might very well turn a blind eye on her modish little ways and that "high art" of hers. All the more as she merely threatened poems and novels, refraining not only from reading them aloud but even from embarking on them. So here they were, awaiting their visitor—not only the violets, but the Finnish maidservant in a bonnet, and much else in the same vein. Zoya Nikolayevna knew when I was due to arrive, and was also aware of my punctuality. So it was hardly by chance that she greeted me in a housecoat (or could it have been a dress of some kind?), reclining on a sofa with a slim English volume in her dainty little hand. Her manner of speaking was at once languid and precise; carried away, however, she launched into the declamatory style I had been led to expect. While remaining "uninfected" myself, I did become a believer in her power to "infect," to cast a spell that might well bring the listener to swooning point. Shchetinkin, who emerged after a time, was his usual charming self but said little. Only seeing me out to the lobby and promising to drop by some time soon did he once again smile his bold, carefree smile.

There was something about the young couple's hospitality I didn't care for much. The violets, the housecoat, the sofa, the slim volume, the ready-made "infectiousness"—all this seemed pre-planned and a little ridiculous. But I told myself that, even if it was all mise-en-scène, everyone had a right to present himself in what he considered to be the most favorable light. It is quite possible that I was dissatisfied because I had yet to re-accustom myself to crawling out from my lair. Everything is possible: I soon forgot all about it—all the more as Kostya, dropping round by himself, was the bold, carefree, practical, energetic boy of old. I did not consider it tactful to question him about such a concurrence. Before long, however, fate was to allot me the role not of distant observer but of active participant in a story that, if by no means uninstructive, is perhaps of less than overwhelming interest. And not so much as active participant as counselor or, as they say, "confidant."

Although I had not felt quite at ease on my visit to the young Shchetinkins, and did not intend to become a frequent guest, relations not only with Kostya but with his wife were, on the surface, not in the least impaired. She would often write me letters—in addition to her other gifts, she was the most zealous of correspondents. Shchetinkin himself continued to drop by every so often in order to share his writing—and sometimes his living—plans. One day he turned up with a plea to find him some sort of work. In the light of Kostya's apparent prosperity, this could hardly fail to surprise: why should he be in need of the tedious and not very rewarding translating work that was the only kind I could supply? But I asked no questions, assuming that the family's welfare was exclusively in Zoya Nikolayevna's hands. Was it not entirely natural for a young man to want some cash, however little, of his own? It wasn't very hard for me to arrange, as I could confidently recommend our poet as hardworking, not untalented, conscientious and—this was the main requirement—extremely neat.

Being invited by my new acquaintances on more than one occasion to an informal luncheon at their place, I felt that it would be awkward and rather unfriendly never to respond to their apparently sincere amicability. They could not have expected much profit or entertainment from my acquaintance—so these people liked me simply because they liked me. Such ungrounded sentiments are often, even usually, fragile, subject as they are to fate's vagaries and caprices. I am even inclined to suppose that when they do turn out to be lasting, they are not really ungrounded, their apparent lack of foundation concealing some base that may well be trifling and silly—therefore ineradicable. But I didn't give it much thought before leaving for distant Vasilevsky Island. The days were growing longer, and a ruddy dusk was still aglow in the Shchetinkins' rooms when I was welcomed by Zoya Nikolayevna and Kostya. The "informal" fare was choice enough, having obviously been given careful consideration—which, incidentally, my hosts made no effort to conceal. But if a certain bourgeois luxuriance (pleasant, and, I should add, not in the least hard to put up with) was apparent in the surroundings, the menu and the decorum of the maidservant, the talk was affable and unconstrained, with a due measure of philosophizing. Judgment was passed on the present condition of our fraternity, especially on the so-called Modernists. It was Mme. Shchetinkina who expressed the most pessimistic view of the subject. According to her, whatever our endeavors, no one had the slightest interest in us, we could not expect to meet with understanding, we were virtually condemned to the existence of parasites, if not to death from starvation. We were, the lot of us, "madmen," "seers" and something else I can't quite remember. According to her, we had no right to exist, to put our clothes on, to behave like everyone else, if such was our fancy (taking account of the proffered fare, this last was of a particular piquancy). It was a familiar enough harangue, if somewhat unexpected on the lips of a literary lady from our own camp. Seeing that the shrinking Kostya was somewhat distressed by Zoya Nikolayevna's eloquence, I began by attempting to refute her to the best of my ability and in what I considered to be a seemly manner. Then, concluding that it would be preferable to turn the conversation to more agreeable topics, I spoke of Konstantin Petrovich's work. Brightening a little, he responded that as soon as he had finished the translation I had obtained for him he would get down to other things. Paying no attention to her husband's words, Zoya Nikolayevna interrupted him and turned to me with an enthusiastic account of our poet's latest conception, of which he himself had yet to utter a word. Its theme was of the utmost sublimity, semi-theosophical, semi-abstract—better suited to the speaker herself than to Shchetinkin, who was blushing like a schoolboy. Almost regretfully I turned to him for elucidation, but he hastened to confirm the information conveyed by his wife. At this point, assuming that he had something prepared, I naturally asked him to give us a reading. He complied with some reluctance, saying that the piece was not going at all well, that he had serious misgivings about it. At Zoya Nikolayevna's insistence, however, he did read a few excerpts, and they inspired me with sad thoughts. I would never have guessed that this nebulous concoction belonged to our friend—it was not, of course, devoid of talent—unpredictable images and rhymes, the odd amusing idea glinting here and there, but it failed to establish any dominant mood, it was neither fish, fowl, nor good red herring, affording displeasure rather than delight. It was apparent that Kostya was "puffing out," as the French say, his own graceful and delicate voice, and what resulted was both comic and pathetic. Him, needless to say, I did not inform of this, giving his verse an evasive appraisal. As if he understood my thoughts, Kostya kept a guilty silence when Zoya Nikolayevna started to demand greater enthusiasm from me. Then, of course, came predictable accusations of snobbery and lack of concern; ultimately we all stood accused of cold-blooded heartlessness, of not knowing what inspiration was—and the culprit for all this turned out to be, for some reason, St. Petersburg.

Finally I brought out:

"Everything you say, Zoya Nikolayevna, may very well be true, but you see before you a genuine unfeeling Petersburger, and this is poetry I don't much care for. I'm also a little annoyed—having the highest regard for Konstantin Petrovich and his talent."

With a defiant smirk the lady asked:

"What is it you don't like?"

"It's only that this is completely unsuited to Konstantin Petrovich."

"You might well be wrong."

"Of course I might—in which case it's even more annoying."

"Why is that?"

"Well, because Konstantin Petrovich has a talent that is rare—both in its power and originality."

"But it can still broaden and deepen."

"Of course it can. But if everyone pulls at a piece of elastic, it will either break or lose its resilience, which is to say, it will no longer be elastic."

To this my interlocutor responded with a contemptuous silence and offered me a cigarette. For several minutes no one said anything, and the silence became very uncomfortable. I hastened to finish my liqueur and began to take my leave, indicating that it behooved the master of the house to get down to his translating: we'd had a pleasant lunch, but it was time stolen from work—and we shouldn't be such loafers as to waste an evening in gossip as well. The lady frowned and said:

"Oh, this wretched translating ... Work isn't always useful, you know; some conversations are more important and more productive than any work."

In these last words I sensed both hint and challenge; not having the slightest desire to take up the latter, I remarked after a silence:

"What can you have against Konstantin Petrovich's translating?"

"I think Kostya ought to be spending his time on something entirely different. This translating only confirms my opinion that no one wants to know us in our present circumstances—and we are compelled to resort to such means: you compose all kinds of music for plays, someone else writes articles and Kostya translates—just to get a foot in the door. But do what we may, we still can't make it, we can't, we can't."

It was true that, having some knowledge of music, I have occasionally, at the request of friends, composed for plays, little foreseeing the grave accusations this would bring down on my head. I started to make a rejoinder, and the altercation would have been protracted had it not been for the arrival of two maiden ladies who had come to see Zoya Nikolayevna with the aim of becoming "infected." On our way to the lobby, I said to Kostya:

"Why did you take this translating on if Zoya Nikolayevna finds it so objectionable?"

He replied that it was for the money.

"But surely you're comfortably off," I indicated the decor complete with violets.

"It's for these very comforts that money is needed."

Now I understood that my suppositions concerning the vice-gubernatorial provenance of many an agreeable item were unfounded. I took my leave of Shchetinkin, wishing him success in his endeavors. His response was to the effect that Zoya Nikolayevna could hardly be expected to exempt him from attending "infection" rituals for the sake of such trivialities as the maintenance of the violets in the lobby as well as an impeccable Finnish maidservant.

I had been out of sorts, so the two of us abstained that evening from getting a foot in any door. I don't know how Shchetinkin spent his evening, but I paid a call on an old friend of mine, a well-known artist, at whose dwelling a close-knit yet diverse company had gathered: another writer, two artists, a musician, a civil servant with the ministry of court, and three young army officers. In this milieu people felt no need to be "seers," "madmen" and "freaks." Amidst singing, joking and lively conversation I soon regained my composure. Returning home, I was once more in a condition, eagerly and boldly, to go about the shameful business of "getting a foot in the door"—which is to say, to the penning of a long delayed and hastily assembled item in a style far from exalted. I must admit to grumbling a little at folk who, for all their concern with my diet, had paid not the slightest heed to the conversational menu, regaling the imprudent visitor with highfalutin but indigestible matter while taking no account of the normal process of intellectual digestion. Such conduct is unsociable and discourteous, not to say unhygienic. Table talk has long been recognized as a blithe and genial commodity. To confirm such a thesis, it is the custom in monasteries to read the "Prologue" at table. Of all the books available to the brethren, the "Prologue" undoubtedly makes the lightest and, if you like, most piquant reading: I am tempted to call it a spiritual "Decameron." Such was the grumble I leveled at high-arty Zoya, pitying the happy-go-lucky Kostya who had been dragged up by the ears to lofty heights where he was beginning to gasp for breath. Having had my grumble I naturally forgot all about it. If Zoya was dissatisfied with me, she seemed no less well-disposed on future encounters, reproaching me for my neglect of them and so on—in a manner not unusual among good friends. I was held by common acquaintances to be the person closest to the Shchetinkins.

In such a way a good number of weeks passed. I saw my Vasilevsky Island acquaintances neither often nor seldom; I avoided argument and, generally speaking, thought it tactful to display less interest in Kostya's fate, what path his poetry was taking, than was really the case. Shchetinkin handed in his translation and failed to apply—to me at any rate—for more work.

That year much water flowed under the bridge in a short time, and any affair of no immediate concern tended to retreat into the background. My friend, the one who had been so long confined to a military school hospital, went away; my nephew Sergei Auslender also departed—for Florence. Seeing him off to the station—seeing people off is a bad habit of mine—I was doubly disconsolate, parting from one of the few people close to me, and revisited by memories of Italy, particularly of Florence, where I had spent many months in the company of a stern but cheerful canon who flourishes to this very day. Springtime melancholy and foreboding were in the air (according to the calendar, spring had begun a while back). I was in no mood to go home, and decided to wander about for a bit before shutting myself up in my rooms. So there I was, shuffling down Shpalernaya Street, making the transition from daydreams of Italy to planning what I would do if only I were fifteen years younger and had an income of five hundred thousand a month. My head was in such an idiotically sentimental state that I was almost sorry to run into Kuskov, who latched onto me as a fellow wanderer, contriving to get himself past my front door. Kuskov was a warm-hearted fusspot—a way of saying he liked meddling in other people's affairs more than was necessary; not so much to offer practical help (which he did with the greatest reluctance) as much as advice and sympathy. The remarkable energy displayed by Kuskov in enterprises of this nature resulted in an unusually extensive knowledge of matters that did not concern him. Catching sight of me that evening, he immediately went into action, fishing for infor-

mation—where had I been?—intermingling with this a yarn
about the Shchetinkins (he knew me to be a friend of theirs).
Somehow he arrived at the unpredictable conclusion that
Zoya Nikolayevna also ought to be off on her travels—in her
case, to Rome. I won't conceal that I found all this a little tedious, and my response to Kuskov's fussing was less than po-
lite: it would do Zoya Nikolayevna no harm to take a trip well
beyond the bounds of Rome. My interlocutor either failed, or
did not choose to notice my tone, starting then and there to
conjecture means of financing the excursion, thus considerably enlivening my attention. I was especially struck by his
knowledge, precise and exceedingly thorough, of the finan-
cial circumstances of the vice-governor's daughter, not so
much by the knowledge itself as—again—by the conclusions
he drew from it, which unexpectedly brought me into the
picture. What follows is a résumé of Kuskov's remarks. The
Shchetinkins had absolutely no source of income but Konstantin Petrovich's literary earnings. Although Zoya Nikolayevna did have her own considerable share in the estate of
her brothers and her sister, she had neither demanded her
portion nor even drawn the interest, which, in view of her
good relations with her kin, would not have been difficult.
How this had come about was unfathomable. My informant
saw in this a special kind of tact, while I was more inclined
to interpret it as some kind of inexplicable pride. Of course,
all this was formulated in different terms, being expounded
in an exceedingly agitated and unsystematic way. To me, apparently, would fall the mission of discussing this subject
with a certain person and making her, so to speak, see reason. In response to my rebuffs, Kuskov, rumpling his ashen
shock of hair, argued that I, being, as he put it, their closest
friend, shouldn't find this so hard to do—and Konstantin Petrovich really was in a fix. It all seemed a bit absurd to me:
the violets and the straitened circumstances and the fancy
clothes and the dissatisfaction with translating. And I'm
leaving out theoretical considerations as they hardly ever
coincide with practical ones. Ever in search of rational
causes—or at least of ones accessible to reason—for all
kinds of phenomena, I decided that, having a certain sum at
their disposal, the Shchetinkins had set themselves up,
dressed themselves up, and had then run aground. Not exactly prudent, of course, but understandable. I flatly refused
to talk to Zoya concerning her share of the family estate, de-

ciding instead to find her some kind of teaching job, one that
would take account of her "gift of tongues." I took no special
steps, but ever here, there and everywhere, kept Kostya's
wife in mind. In this way I stumbled across something I
judged appropriate. Certain acquaintances of mine, friends
of my father, had two daughters—princesses—who were no
fools, needing not so much an instructress as an older female
friend to help with their intellectual development. The family itself, of ancient lineage, was rich and hospitable in the
Russian style. To these it was I wished to direct Zoya Nikolayevna, as I wrote to her in a letter couched in the following
terms: such an arrangement would be more advantageous to
the prince's young daughters than to Zoya Nikolayevna herself. A few days later I received a note inviting me to pay a
visit to Vasilevsky Island, a postscript announcing: "The two
of us will be by ourselves." Why it was she considered it necessary for the two of us to be secluded, I couldn't quite conjecture, but I set off without fail. This time Zoya, lying on the
same sofa, was wearing a formal dress and held in her hands
not a slim English volume but some kind of document (either
a bill or an invoice), which on my appearance she hastened
to thrust into a torn, grey envelope.

She was straightforward, starting without preamble:

"I am very grateful to you, Mikhail Alekseyevich, but I
don't intend to take a position with those friends of yours."

"May I ask why not?"

"I don't have the time."

I must admit that, being completely unprepared for such
a response, I made a humble bow. Wishing to be of genuine
service rather than merely to fulfill an obligation, I began
anew:

"Zoya Nikolayevna, may I speak to you frankly, as to a
friend?"

"Please do," she responded, not altogether invitingly.

"I would like to be of genuine assistance, being extremely
attached to both you and Konstantin Petrovich. If you will
pardon the indiscretion: are you really as busy as you say?
Don't you need some extra source of income?"

Zoya Nikolayevna got to her feet, took a few steps, sat down
again, pressing her palms to her temples as if they were chill.
I had never seen her before in so agitated a condition. At last
she said:

"I will be equally frank with you, Mikhail Alekseyevich;

your surmise is correct: things are going very badly with us. You remember how you attacked me when I said that the modern writers who haven't been able to catch the mood of the crowd are condemned to a pitiful existence. Well, now I find my words confirmed. You're looking at the decor? Of course, we don't live in a cellar, and we don't go about in rags—that I couldn't endure—but all the same this is poverty, utter destitution! I am grateful to you for wanting to help us, but I really cannot accept your offer. I cannot give up the work to which I am devoted, that I would hold it a sin to renounce—even if such renunciation were to lead to prosperity—my own work and that of those dear to me."

"So what is to be done now?" I asked, as if lost in thought.

"Indeed, what is to be done?" she repeated, pressing her palms to her icy temples. "I could, of course, turn to my relatives, even demand my share of the estate. But that also I cannot, I do not wish to do."

By saying this, she untied my hands: I was able to raise the question that previously, before this openness, I would not have dared to venture:

"Why don't you ask for the share to which you are entitled so that you can freely devote yourself to your vocation?"

Since she remained silent, I repeated, as gently as I could:

"Why not do that? You must admit that pride would be unsuitable here, even if it could be interpreted as some kind of liberalism. Forgive me for saying this, but it weighs heavy on your husband. It is hardly a good thing to play the liberal at someone else's expense."

"You're right, of course, but I can't bring myself to do that. It is something higher than I am."

I saw that there was nothing I could do, and asked in parting:

"I will be tactless to the end and express a desire to find out why it was you wanted this conversation to be without witnesses. Perhaps there is something else you want to say to me?"

"You've guessed . . ." she responded, and fell silent.

"What exactly?"

As if plucking up courage, she said simply and precisely:

"Get me ten thousand on a three-year loan—at low interest, of course."

I had thought there was nothing that would come as a surprise—but this I was not expecting. I responded with un-feigned amazement:

"What do you mean, Zoya Nikolayevna? Where could I possibly find so much money?"

"So there's nowhere you could get it?" she asked, screwing up her eyes.

Making a swift mental survey of all the possibilities, I responded in the negative.

"What is to be done, then? If it's impossible, it's impossible! And nothing will be of help anyhow!" So saying, she rang the bell for tea to be served.

The same bonneted maidservant brought us English biscuits, muskmelon preserve and steaming cups of tea, while Zoya Nikolayevna, continuing to press her temples, repeated, this time in Parisian dialect:

"Beggars, that's what we are—literally beggars!"

In taking my leave, I asked her once again to consider claiming her share of the estate. According to my calculations, it would have amounted to a sum of about fifty thousand. Zoya, without a word, shook her head in refusal. So it was I left without accomplishing my mission. Again I was filled with vexation at the strange pride of this governor's daughter (even if her father had been no more than a vice-governor).

I saw no more of the Shchetinkins until the summer after that. At the end of June I set off for Novgorod province, where I remained until well into autumn, even intending to winter there. There it was, amidst transparent lakes, a sky transparent with an autumnal transparency, amidst the variegated hues of September woods, the glassy silence of the air, that I was startled by a letter from Kuskov informing me—completely without explanation—that Kostya Shchetinkin had shot himself.

"What? Why? How did it happen?"

That same evening I quickly set off by horse-drawn carriage for a seven-hour train journey, pondering the whole way how such a misfortune could have come to pass. Say what you will, it is hard enough to determine the reasons behind the actions of a living man, let alone those of a dead one. All the conjectures of the people surrounding him are no more than conjectures. If they do present any interest, it is only touching the concerns of those investigating the matter, not those of the dead man.

Neither was I, twisting and turning seven hours long on my sleeping-car mattress, able to come up with anything apart from what I already knew.

I knew Kostya and I knew his art; I'd also had time enough to take the measure of Zoya Nikolayevna. Their incompatibility was obvious, as was their "destitution"; Kostya's hesitations, his stumblings and ultimate collapse instead of the illumination one would have hoped for, had been brought about by two conflicting outlooks— all that was comprehensible to any unbiased observer. But surely these woes were remediable by means other than a gunshot.

However this may have been, it was not without bitterness and disquiet that I passed through the portal of the church where poor Shchetinkin received the last rites. Kuskov had made the arrangements, paying his deceased comrade a final debt of fuss and bother. Among those present were not only close relatives and friends; predictably, it was only around the coffin that an appropriate decorum was maintained. Among the bystanders, where I was, "tittle-tattle" was prevalent.

Kuskov was defending Zoya from the censure of another acquaintance, who maintained that it was her "infectiousness" that had done Kostya in.

A half-deaf old woman, pushing her way forward to pay her respects to the dead, came to a puzzled halt:

". . . just don't get it . . . first he's the dear departed, then all of a sudden he's infectious?"

I calmed her down, and she shuffled on. Then I stepped onto the porch, took a look at the yellow trees, at the deep blue of the sky that day, carried my flowers to the open grave, and left without seeing Zoya Nikolayevna.

Recently I heard that Zoya Nikolayevna is carrying on her mission of "infection" in other circles. There is growing report of literary works, still unseen, in the process of composition. Kostya's passing she regrets mainly because he never finished that notorious epic of his, fragments from which he had read to us at that luncheon.

I make no generalizations, merely recounting what occurred. I leave it to the reader to draw his own conclusions—unless he finds it too tedious.

All things pass, of course, and to all things man grows accustomed; but now I can far better understand the words of St. Ephraim the Syrian: "Give not unto me a spirit of idleness, of despondency, of lust for power." From such a spirit proceeds vain utterance, exalted and despondent, proceeds rejection of life with its labors and joys.

August, 1910

Underground Streams

". . . ALL INSTRUCTORS WILL BE PARTICIPATING"—SUDDENLY ONE leg flies up in the air, another is quick to follow, an uncommonly capacious galosh artlessly depicts a zeppelin against the fragile blue of March, while Strukov's torso senses a puddle's cold through an old overcoat. Absorbed in an advertisement for a skating rink, he hardly had time to cast a reproachful glance at the ice-covered bulge that had tripped him up. An insufficiency of passersby did not permit Strukov's fall to develop into a roadside spectacle. The urchins who sold cigarettes were a long way off, but a bunch of businesslike personages did momentarily cease uttering the barbaric names of various institutions before hastening on their way. An old woman carrying a sack gave voice to a few sympathetic cusswords, prophesying, somewhat in the manner of Merezhkovsky, the impending collapse of the entire city of St. Petersburg.

Pavel Nikolayevich was brushing himself down without retreating from the constantly dripping water when he heard words obviously addressed to himself:

"The water's dripping on you—and there you are standing in a puddle. Here's your other galosh."

A lady still young in years was approaching him, the dirty galosh that had flown from his foot dangling from her wary hand. A confused Strukov dragged a foot through the water in an attempt to click his heels and—who knows why?—introduced himself. The lady smiled and said:

"It doesn't matter. I don't mean your being Strukov, Pavel Nikolayevich, but your falling down."

"To you, of course, it doesn't matter."

"And it shouldn't to you either—or not very much. Unpleasant—it's true, but it could hardly be said to matter. Petersburg won't collapse as a result. Only don't clean your clothes before they dry out. Good bye."

For some reason, Strukov examined and committed the

woman's perfectly ordinary features to memory; the low, somewhat husky voice he remembered without effort. This rather humiliating encounter was not, he sensed, the beginning of a romance—nothing could have been further from his thoughts.

*   *   *

For all his idyllic surname, Maksim Ivanovich Krylechkin was an old man of towering height who, owing to his advanced years, put one in mind of a storm-damaged frigate. This impression was confirmed by his manner of drifting down the street—shortsighted, insensible of his surroundings, he would stumble and come to a halt with every step, appareled in a cape and carrying a broken umbrella, books stuffed randomly into every available pocket. A booklover from his early days, he had to barter goods near Vladimirskaya church when his store had been closed down, and now he was trading in a cooperative nominally run by three young writers. Authors of little books of verse, they understood business to the same extent as Maksim Ivanovich Gothic grammar. Once in a while, let's say three times a year, he would call on Strukov for a cup of tea. Having known Strukov since his schooldays, Krylechkin addressed his friend with the familiarity of an old man.

Knowing Pavel Nikolayevich to be a great connoisseur of the mystical writings published by the Novikov circle in the late eighteenth and early nineteenth centuries, on this occasion Krylechkin had brought a present with him—a rather rare edition of *The Journey of Young Kostis*.

"Do take it. Don't worry, you won't ruin me. Four pages are missing and the bookbinder managed to mix up twenty others. You won't sell it to a book-fancier or a collector, and folks who aren't book-fanciers won't even give it a glance. You're a man who reads books, you don't keep them just for show; you'll understand it, even with four pages missing. I got it for almost nothing from a lady I know—Petrova by name, Maria Rodionovna. Ever heard of her?"

Never having heard of Maria Rodionovna Petrova, Strukov rendered thanks for the book and treated Krylechkin to the kind of American tea that has to be boiled rather than made in the traditional manner. But the old booklover again began talking of Maria Rodionovna, even recounting certain epi-

sodes of her biography he happened to know. Four years before, apparently, Petrova's husband had been mistakenly
executed in place of another prisoner, a burglar also called
Petrov. This latter had soon been released, the charge
against Maria Rodionovna's husband not being a serious
one. The burglar had the effrontery to show up at the widow's apartment, begging her not to give him away: by doing
so she would hardly resurrect her husband, but for the burglar it would be the end. For some inexplicable reason, Petrova agreed to his request, which was not difficult to do
since the Petrovs were newcomers and hardly anyone had
known her late husband. But rumor of this seeped through
somehow, even getting as far as Maksim Ivanovich, who was
not among the Petrovs' close acquaintances. The old man re-
counted the episode simply, without any attempt at psycho-
logical interpretation, just as he would have spoken of a
robbery, a new tariff or a cold spring.

"Is she living in her apartment with this burglar as if he
were her husband?"

"No, how can you say that! He left immediately—they say
he bowed right down to her feet."

"And so they haven't seen each other since then?"

"Well, I don't know about that. They say he calls round
from time to time. And he didn't even turn out to be a real
burglar."

"What was he then?"

"Goodness only knows. Lots of folk are called Petrov."

"It is strange all the same."

"An odd one she is, that Maria Rodionovna. Always happy.
Even these days. And that after losing what seemed to be all
she had. And don't you go thinking that she's some kind of . . .
Petrov's a common name, of course, but do you know what
her name was before she got married, when she was a young
miss? Just saying it took your breath away, such a fine one it
was. And it doesn't make a bit of difference, she's just the
way she is."

Krylechkin began to take his leave, searching for the sack
he always carried on his back just in case. This tale of people
completely unknown to him aroused Strukov's lively interest, and he eagerly accepted the booklover's invitation to
call on Petrova with him next morning just to take a look at
any books she might have left.

*   *   *

One had to go through the kitchen. According to habits born of cold winters and reduced living quarters, the place was crowded with people and remnants of unwanted furniture. In the space between the windows there was even an ancient English grandfather clock, which slowly and sedately struck eleven as the visitors stepped into steam and fumes. Three women and a teenager with a bag of old painted planks were holding up banknotes to the light; paying the visitors almost no attention, they directed them to the apartment. At virtually the same moment a young lady appeared from a narrow corridor. Strukov immediately recognized her. She it was who had assured him a few days earlier that falling down in a puddle didn't matter. She hastily led them to a spacious room, which was, judging by the absence of long pipes for heating, uninhabited. Pointing to the dusty bookshelves, she said:

"Be so kind, Maksim Ivanovich, as to take a look at the books without me. If you do find something interesting, just put it to one side. We'll agree on a price. I'm so busy, you know. Every minute has to be accounted for. What with all this work, and housekeeping too, time simply flies. One fine morning I'll wake up and find myself an old woman before I know it."

"Come on, it's early for you to be thinking of old age."

"I don't think of it and, besides, it doesn't frighten me in the least."

"How brave you are!"

Maria Rodionovna frowned slightly and pronounced in a more heartfelt tone:

"Brave? What kind of bravery do you call that? It's true that a lot of stupid things I used to find unbearable don't frighten me anymore. But there's no great merit in that."

"Yes, life teaches us many lessons."

"And the Lord be thanked that it does."

For some reason Strukov got into the conversation:

"We've met, you know—I even introduced myself. Strukov, Pavel Nikolayevich."

"Probably it was a long time ago, somewhere in the provinces."

By no means embarrassed, Petrova reluctantly examined the purchaser more closely.

"Maybe she's afraid of me having known her husband," thought Strukov, and hurriedly added:

"Just four days ago, on Basseinaya Street."

"Basseinaya Street?"

"Yes, I was the one who, if you'll pardon the expression, fell down in a puddle."

"Oh yes, you did look a bit pathetic. So we're old friends," concluded the lady of the house gaily, holding out a hand. As he kissed the extended hand, a strange certainty that this was neither the beginning nor the continuation of a romance flashed through Pavel Nikolayevich's mind.

* * *

In an odd volume of Voltaire, Strukov found a notebook covered in tiny handwriting. Unthinkingly he began to read, collecting himself only when he had finished. Only then did he understand that this was not a diary a couple of centuries old, but a number of observations touching on recent years, made in all likelihood by Maria Rodionovna herself. He then turned his attention to the words that stood at the top of the notebook's first page:

"To be read after my death."

But who could the intended reader be? Assuredly not he, not Pavel Nikolayevich Strukov. He felt dreadfully uneasy, but the deed was done. To run to her straightaway or to conceal everything? Perhaps she had discovered the notebook's absence and, not knowing into whose hands it had fallen, would have become unduly worried. The notebook contained fragments of a diary, of meditations, as well as passages copied out of books, most frequently (or so it seemed to Strukov) from the very same *Journey of Young Kostis*, which had apparently been read attentively during these last years.

But why "after my death"? What had compelled the young woman to seek such a way out of so desperate a situation, and what had restrained her?

* * *

Fragments from a notebook. Yes, that must be it. Apparently written between 1918 and 1921. Perhaps Strukov didn't remember the exact order of these manuscript fragments, but only the order they had assumed in his head, illuminating their author. He may well have omitted the scenes that were most dramatic, the thoughts that were most significant, but he had good reason to remember what he did. Beneath these scattered fragments some subterranean passage of the soul was clear to him.

* * *

"Of course, I didn't remember his face, and it was only at our third or fourth encounter that I took a good look at him. A bit rough in appearance, he was handsome and well built. The military cut of his clothes ("commissar-style," as they say these days) suited him, as it does any young man (ridiculous, of course, that Yakov Davydovich has taken it into his head to force himself into a service jacket at the age of forty-five).

But all the same I find it painful to meet him.

He's called Arkady—a tasteless sort of name somehow. It's a strange situation, however you look at it: very romantic but devoid of romance."

* * *

"A good thing that I was a young lady from the country and never despised physical exercise. The nonsense they stuffed our heads with!"

* * *

"At first I used to dream of my favorite dishes, but I don't anymore. I eat everything. If I get the chance I treat myself to the odd tasty morsel, but I don't suffer from lack of them. That's the way it is with everything. It isn't asceticism, but rather a more accurate assessment of our needs; things that used to occupy first place have now shifted to tenth or even twentieth. Our physical needs can be reduced to a minimum. That's tremendously liberating. A pity I've been brought to it by necessity—but a bargain is a bargain."

* * *

"Just to maintain a bold and positive attitude—and then the game is won. And who would I frighten anyway with my anger or my faintheartedness?"

*   *   *

"The institution where I work has a monstrous name, but these are the sort of words I've seen in the book of telegraph abbreviations. There is efficiency in that, of course. I remember that Khlebnikov has a theory that numbers are going to be introduced for everyday use and for business purposes, while words in their essential meaning will be reserved for poetry alone."

*   *   *

"A letter from Lydia, she's in Shanghai. Some are in Prague, some are in Zurich, London, Tokyo. We are scattered wide, as the Bible has it, and the world is as small as it was in the eighteenth century. Citizens of the entire world. Aleksei Mikhailovich is terribly homesick in Berlin. I'm thinking: that's the way Russians are. But that too is prejudice. A native land is a language, a few customs, a climate and a landscape."

*   *   *

Excerpt from *The Journey of Young Kostis*:

The spirit of evil spoke once more: "For this purpose, it has been my endeavor first of all to divide mankind into as many peoples as possible. Everywhere did I awaken national pride, so that one nation might hate and oppress another. Everywhere did I endeavor to introduce different manners, different opinions, different customs, different apparel . . . When, in such a way, I had set apart from each other the nations that were intended to form a single community, I then sowed discord within each nation. Each did I divide into classes, thus poisoning every heart with pride, since one caste held itself superior to another, and dissension multiplied. By divergence of opinion did I turn mankind away from reason and from the path of truth. By means of overweening self-love—from love of union. By means of avarice—from social wellbeing."

In general, men's bodily parts are identical, as are their feelings, as are their needs. It is therefore needful that they be joined in equality of esteem, in equality of love and in equality of advantage. Equality of esteem among all humankind should serve as a law to guide your intelligence, equality of love should serve as guide to your heart; equality of profit should serve as guide to your actions and their object.

*   *   *

"These are, of course, the commonplaces of eighteenth century enlightenment, but there is truth in them, and I understand Catherine the Great's persecution."

*   *   *

"The earthly paradise is a senseless dream—but it would seem to be an ineradicable one in man."

*   *   *

"In my childhood we had a lizard. At the appropriate time it would change its skin. You had to see it twisting about, thrashing with its tail, rubbing itself against the walls of its box; the old skin would split, and dry, ring-shaped fragments would go flying in all directions until—debonair, youth restored—it would gleam a brilliant emerald. From us too, sometimes not without our own efforts, all kinds of absurd and ridiculous prejudices and addictions can fall away one by one."

*   *   *

"Many things are dear to me, and were I all of a sudden to find myself with Lydia in Shanghai, I would sit, not without pleasure, in a restaurant gazing at the rosy sea in the company of sailors from every land. But I would soon get bored with that. I know now that there is more to life, that this is not what matters—in the same way as I know that the a country's culture is not to be measured by the condition of its roads. Not even a tiny plot of heaven can be fenced off for private use."

*   *   *

"Was it not Arkady who gave the jolt that brought about this rebirth of mine? Perhaps it was—as well as my husband's death, not to mention more general reasons. A strange thing about Arkady (and not just him, but many other people, too), is the appetite he has for life, one that might well be understood in a twenty-year-old. But he squanders it on such trivialities: on shoes, on walking sticks, on living in style, on theater. And he's serious about all this. He squanders money on exactly the kind of things I'm managing to rid myself of. But one can't do without love of life, one really can't. Perhaps in some different form, something more spiritual—could that be it? This delight in material blessings, the very things that used to be unavailable to him—maybe it will pass. To what catastrophe has blind materialism led Western Europe? Just think of that."

*   *   *

"And then I ceased to consider my own esteemed personage the navel of the earth, and from that I gained only benefit. This is what is known as 'Virtue Rewarded' ...."

*   *   *

All the same, Strukov took the notebook to Maria Rodionovna. She seemed a little embarrassed, thanked him, and asked:

"Did you read it?"

"I must confess that I did."

"Well, it can't be helped. You weren't to know it was secret."

"And I'm very grateful to you."

"For the pleasure afforded?"

"I'm not joking. You're astonishing."

Wrinkling her grey eyes, Petrova said softly:

"But please don't take all this as a chapter from a novel, especially as my husband turned out to be alive, and is soon coming back from the camp."

"But what about Arkady?"

"What has Arkady got to do with it? It isn't a novel, it's real life. Instead of shooting my husband, they sentenced him to hard labor, even though the crime had been committed by someone with the same name. And now my husband is a free man. I've waited for him faithfully and I've become a better person, too—better adapted, if you like."

Strukov suddenly remembered:

"Maria Rodionovna, may I ask you a question?"

"By all means. It makes no difference, the two of us are unlikely ever to meet again."

"Why are those notes of yours written as if in anticipation of death? Even the inscription on them seems to say that."

"That's the way I thought it was going to be. But they turned out to be 'notes in anticipation of life.' I intend to live—yes, very much so."

After a silence she began again:

"I too will ask a question in parting, a simpler one: have you ever been to the province of Olonets?"

"No, I haven't."

"It is a land of wonders, a land of sorcerers. There are rivers, streams there that disappear beneath the soil, spurting forth again fresh and unknown in meadowlands many miles away. That's how I am, too. Perhaps I'm under the earth now, blindly digging. But I believe that the valley where my faithful waves break through will be cool and fragrant."

1922

Literary Manifestoes

Concerning Beautiful Clarity

Remarks on Prose

When solid elements joined to form dry land, and waters girded the earth with seas, spreading over it in rivers and lakes, then the world first emerged from the condition of chaos, above which moved the dividing Spirit of God. And then—by delimitation, by clear furrows—came into being a complex and beautiful world, accepting or not accepting which, artists, each in his own way, strive to know, to see and to imprint.

In the life of every man there come moments when, as a child, he will suddenly say: "I and chair," "I and cat," "I and ball"; later, being a full-grown man: "I and the world." Whatever his future attitude toward the world, this moment of division is always a profound turning point.

In similar stages does art periodically proceed, now measuring out, distributing and fashioning its lode; now forms that have been brought to perfection are broken up by a fresh wave of chaotic forces, a new barbaric invasion.

But on looking about us, we see that the creative periods striving toward clarity stand as beacons pointing the way to a single goal, and the thrust of a destructive tide can only lend new sheen to eternal stones and add new gems to the treasure house it has endeavored to destroy.

There are artists who bring to mankind the chaos, bewildered horror and fragmentation of their own spirit, and there are others who endow the world with their own harmony. There is no particular need to say how much the latter, assuming equivalence of talent, are superior to the former, how much greater is their healing power. It is not difficult to surmise why, in a troubled age, authors who lay bare their ulcers harrow the nerves, even if not "setting on fire" the hearts of masochistic listeners. Without pausing to examine the fact that his aesthetic, moral and religious duty constrains a man (and an artist in particular) to seek and to find within himself peace, in his own soul and with the world, we consider it indisputable that the work of even the most unreconciled, unclear and amorphous writer is subject to the laws of lucid harmony and architectonics. Even the most freakish, obscure and gloomy inventions of Edgar Poe, the unbridled fantasies of Hoffmann are especially dear to us precisely because they are embodied in crystal form. What is to be said of a humdrum Moscow anecdote arrayed in apparel so somber, unintelligible, cosmic that the rare line making sense is greeted as a long-lost friend? Would not someone inclined to suspicion say that the author is purposely spreading murk lest we understand that there is nothing worth understanding? This discrepancy between form and content, absence of contour, needless blur and acrobatic syntax could be called by a not very pretty name . . . We will affix a modest label—tastelessness.

Let your soul be whole or let it be cloven, your perception of the world mystical, realistic, skeptical or even idealistic (should you be so unfortunate); let your creative devices be impressionistic, realistic, naturalistic; the content lyrical or narrative; let there be mood, impression, whatever you like, only, I implore you, be logical—may I be forgiven this cry from the heart!—logical in design, construction, syntax.

Disregard (unintentional) of logic is so alien to human nature, that if you were forced to name ten objects unconnected with each other, you would hardly be able to do so. An interesting inference might be drawn if you copied out of a poem only the nouns: it would seem to us to be beyond doubt that the reason for semantic distance from one word to another lies in the circuitous path of thought and, consequently, in the verse's density, and not at all in the absence of logical dependence. Even less tolerable, particularly in prose, is a similar absence of logic in form; it is least tolerable in the detail, in the construction of periods and phrases. One would like to write out in letters of gold the scene from *Le bourgeois gentilhomme* on the wall of an "academy of prose," if we had such a thing:

TEACHER OF PHILOSOPHY: First of all, you can keep your words in the order that you have: "Beautiful Marquise, your beautiful eyes make me die of love." Or: "Of love make me die, beautiful Marquise, your beautiful eyes." Or:

"Your beautiful eyes of love make me, beautiful Marquise,
die." Or: "To die of love, beautiful Marquise, make me
your beautiful eyes." Or: "Your eyes beautiful of love me
make, beautiful Marquise, die." Or: "To die your beautiful
eyes, beautiful Marquise, of love me make." Or: "Me make
your eyes beautiful die, beautiful Marquise, of love."
M. JOURDAIN. But of all those ways, which is best?
TEACHER OF PHILOSOPHY. The way you said it before:
"Beautiful Marquise, your beautiful eyes make me die of
love."   (Act II, sc. 6)

Oh yes, M. Jourdain, you said your piece very well, just as
it should have been said, although you assure us you've
never been a student!

Perhaps the technique of prose speech is not so well developed as the theory of verse and verse form, but what has
been done for oratorical prose, i.e., declaimed before an audience, may be applied in full measure to words not intended to be read aloud. There we study the composition of
periods, cadences, introductions, conclusions and ornamen-
tation with rhetorical figures. We study, so to speak, the lay-
ing of the stones of the building whose architects we wish to
be; and we must have a sharp eye, a sure hand and a clear
sense of balance, of perspective, of elegance to attain the desired result. It is essential that the structure should not collapse because of a misplaced arch, that detail should be
subordinate to the whole, that the most unsymmetrical and
disturbing project should be realized by deliberate and reg-
ular means. This indeed will be the art of which was said: *ars
longa, vita brevis*. Essential, apart from spontaneous talent
and a firm grasp of material and form, is the correspondence
of the latter with content. A story, by its form, does not ask,
does not even admit exclusively lyrical content, without
something being narrated (not, of course, a story about feeling, about an impression). Still greater is the narrative
element demanded by the novel, nor should it be forgotten
that the Romance lands more than anywhere else were cradle to novella and novel. It was here an Apollonian view
of art developed: delimiting, formative, precise and well-
proportioned. And the models for the story and the novel—
beginning with Apuleius, the Italian and Spanish novelists,
through Abbé Prévost, Lesage, Balzac, Flaubert to Anatole
France and, finally, the matchless Henri de Régnier—must,

of course, be sought in Latin lands. Particularly dear to us is the name of the last of these writers, who is both supremely contemporary and a faultless master of style, giving us no reason to fear that he will encumber the roof of an *Empire* mansion with chimney-pots, or will add a Gothic belltower to a Grecian portico.

We have at last pronounced the word so abused at the present time in both invective and dithyramb—the word "style." Style, stylish, stylizer—these, it would seem, are clearly defined concepts, but nevertheless some kind of confidence trick engendering confusion seems to be in process. When the French call Anatole France a stylist unmatched since Voltaire, they do not, of course, have exclusively in mind his novellas of Italian history. He is everywhere a superb stylist—in articles, in novels of contemporary life, in whatever he touches. This means that he preserves the logic and spirit of the French language in its utmost purity, making cautious innovations, but never venturing beyond the bounds of the language. In this respect Mallarmé is by no means a stylist. To preserve the purity of a language does not mean to deprive it somehow of flesh and blood, to over-polish, to kosher the meat—rather, not to coerce it, but firmly to keep watch over its character, its penchants, its caprices. This may roughly be termed—its grammar (not textbook, but experimental), or logic of native speech. Based on such knowledge, or feeling for language, advances—in the sense of neologisms and syntactical innovations—are possible. From this viewpoint we do not hesitate to apply the name of stylist to Ostrovsky, Pechersky and especially to Leskov—that treasury of Russian speech, who, alongside Dahl's Dictionary, should be a desktop volume. We should wait a little, however, before bestowing the title "stylist" on Andrei Bely, Zinaida Gippius and Aleksei Remizov.

But as soon as we call to mind the saying "the style is the man," we find ourselves ready to put these writers at the top of the list. Clearly some utterly different concept is being defined, and a relatively recent one is here indicated, it being rather difficult to distinguish these novelists from each other by their style. Obviously we are speaking of that individuality of language, that aroma, that je ne sais quoi that should belong to any gifted writer, that ought to be peculiar to any gifted writer, which distinguishes him from another one as do his appearance, the sound of his voice, etc. But if this quality is endemic to all (gifted, deserving) writers, there's no need to underline it, to single it out, and we decline to call a writer who develops "his own" style to the detriment of purity of language a stylist, all the more as both these qualities are perfectly compatible, as is apparent from the examples mentioned above.

A third concept of style, which of late has put down sturdy root in our own Russia, is closely connected with "stylish-ness," "stylization"; on the subject of this last we shall have more to say.

It seems to us that in this case we are concerned with the special, distinct correspondence of the language to the aesthetic and historical significance of a literary work's given form. Just as any kind of subject matter may not be suited to terza rima, to the sonnet, to the rondeau, and artistic tact prompts an appropriate form for every thought, every feeling, so is it even more proper that appropriate language be found for any subject, any age or epoch in a work of prose. Thus Pushkin's language, while continuing to preserve an ir-reproachable purity of Russian speech without losing aroma, somehow alters imperceptibly but unmistakably, de-pending whether the poet is writing "The Queen of Spades," "Scenes from Medieval Times," or the fragment "Caesar was journeying . . ." The same can be said about Leskov. This quality is precious and well-nigh essential to the artist who does not wish to restrict himself to a single orbit, a single pe-riod in his depictions.

This unavoidable and legitimate device (in connection with historicism) caused shortsighted people to confuse it with stylization. Stylization is the transposition of one's own concept to a certain epoch, its embodiment in the appro-priate literary form of a given time. Thus, we include under the heading "stylization" the *Contes drôlatiques* of Balzac, Flaubert's *Trois contes* (but not *Salammbô*, not *La tentation de Saint Antoine*), Henri de Régnier's *Le bon plaisir*, Turgenev's *Song of Triumphant Love*, Leskov's legends, Bryusov's *Fiery Angel*, but not the stories of Sergei Auslender, not Remizov's *Leimonarion*.

In fact these last writers, wishing to make use of certain epochs and adapting their language to this wish, are far from the notion of using ready-made forms, and only those who have never held ancient novellas or genuine apocrypha in their hands could consider these books to represent perfect stylization. Stylization, indeed, might well be considered artistic counterfeiting, an aesthetic game, a *tour de force*, were it not that contemporary writers invest, in spite of themselves, both their love for the antique and their individuality in these forms. It is not by chance they recognize them to be the most suitable for their concepts. This is particularly apparent in *The Fiery Angel*, where thoroughly Bryusovian collisions, Bryusovian language (impeccable Russian) is so amazingly compounded with the German autobiographical short story of the seventeenth century in a form at once accurate and authentic.

To sum up all that has been said, were I permitted to admonish, I would put it like this: "My friend, if you have talent, that is to say—the ability to see the world in your own, new way, an artist's memory, the capacity to distinguish the essential from the incidental, power of true-to-life invention—write logically, preserving the purity of popular speech. Possessing a style of your own, have a clear feeling for the correspondence of a given form to a certain content, and for language appropriate to it. Be a skilled architect in trifling detail as well as in the whole. Be comprehensible in your expressions." But I would whisper in the ear of my dearest friend: "If you be a conscientious artist, pray that your chaos (if you are chaotic) be illumined and ordered, or, in the meantime, hold it in check with lucid form: let a tale tell a story, in the drama let there be action, keep lyricism for verse, love the word as Flaubert did; be economic in means and parsimonious in words, precise and genuine—and you will discover a wonderful secret: beautiful clarity, which I would call "Clarism."

But "the way of art is long, and life is short," and are not all these instructions nothing more than the best of wishes addressed to myself?

1910

Declaration of Emotionalism

1. The essence of art is *to produce a unique and inimitable emotional effect by means of transmission—in a unique and inimitable form—of a unique and inimitable emotional perception.*

2. Creative in itself, *active*—non-abstract—*love* induces creativity.

3. Any manifestation of creativity—be it of love or of life—is linked inextricably with *motion*.

4. Victory over material, over form is the *condition* for the successful creative act—but is not its task or its goal.

5. Emotionalism is aware that the artist's passionate infatuation with the material of his art is only a means of the emotional cognition of the world. The professional experience of the artist creates from this material a form, one that is indispensable for the nation to perceive the artist's way of seeing the world.

6. In dealing with inimitable emotions, with the fleeting moment, with chance, with man, Emotionalism recognizes only the *phenomenal* and the *exceptional*, rejecting *general* types, canons, laws of psychology, history and even those of nature. The only law held to be mandatory by Emotionalism is the law of death.

7. Divine, intuitive, insane *reason* is the guide of the artist's thought; logical, scientific intellect is permissible only in an emotionally altered state. It is then that intellect—being essentially opposed to reason—approaches reason.

8. *Secession* from general laws in favor of inimitable *exaltation* (ecstasy).

9. Neither past nor future exists independently of our present—a present defined emotionally by all of man's spiritual forces, a present that is supremely sacred, a present that is the object of art.

10. Having outgrown, having digested all the sentiments, all the feelings of the old West (France, England, Italy), the old West that suffers from spiritual constipation (for the mo-

tions of spiritual nourishment are identical to those of corporeal sustenance—it is impossible to ingest something new without first expelling superfluous waste), Emotionalism—whose strengthening current is flowing over Russia, Germany and America—strives to formulate the most elementary laws, descrying in lofty simplicity a counterweight to the magnificent forms of the most delightful temptations of Europeanism.

11. Deriving from the individual and inimitable, art extends to the general, the national and the universal. A reversal of this process in unthinkable. Love of humanity is to be discerned in a concrete, particular love, and not vice versa. To take as the point of departure a generalized feeling, a generalized canon, a generalized law is a senseless crime and a lie.

Move on by upward extension, not by downward constriction.

Emotionality as a Basic Element of Art

IT WOULD BE CRIMINAL HYPOCRISY AND INCOMPREHENSIBLE SNOB-bery to be silent concerning the basic foundations of ideology in the arts for fear that they might already be familiar; all the more, as taking a generally admitted premise to be one's starting point, one can arrive at conclusions that are far from being generally accepted. The sun's warmth is a sufficiently known phenomenon, but its uses and effects can be distinguished by an unexpected multiplicity. But in investigating these effects we cannot fail to mention this very warmth of the sun as a phenomenon both commonplace and unworthy of mention. Let us leave such behavior to literary snobs. In addition, basic theses and conditions that seem too elementary are frequently ignored, if only because they must not be allowed to interfere with straying onto a path already known to be a false one, or for specious impostors to be set up in their allegedly vacant place.

However attractive and interesting the manifold stages of the creative process may be, however novel and varied the improvements (or simply changes) in technical devices, it is wrong to allot to them greater significance than they already have. The shifting of the point of balance, without modification of equilibrium, will almost inevitably result in a fall.

It should be established anew that the quintessence of art lies in the production of a singular and unique emotional effect, which is expressed in the singular and unique form of a singular and unique emotional perception.

Each of these three features can, of course, be individually examined, but not one of them can attain its full weight standing alone. Temporal sequence is scarcely possible to violate: attempts to shuffle perception, form, consequence cannot but be fatal. Singularity, uniqueness and emotionality—each of these properties is essential to the creation of a work of art. The connection between the first two, more often than not an unconscious one, is perforce established by the

233

artist; the connection between the second and third, i.e., between the work of art and the emotional effect it produces, is largely dependent on the nature of the spectator. The spectator's or listener's trust in the artist and their receptivity to him facilitate a more powerful impact, although no certain effect can be guaranteed. But if there is an effect, it will assuredly be emotional in nature. Unknown, however, is the sphere of life in which this effect will be produced, over what period of time it will germinate the emotional seed inevitably sown by any work of art. This influence cannot but be a moral one, it must awaken or strengthen the will to live, inducing acceptance of the world, and if not acceptance, then a temporary rejection resulting in a greater affirmation (or at least a temporary repudiation leading to a greater affirmation). This I mention because there does exist a genus of artists who build their art on hatred and denial—which do, of course, have a place among the emotions. But such phenomena cannot be viewed as other than harmful, and must be categorically rejected by a true Emotionalist. At the same time it should not be forgotten that all false art based on denial and hatred, all immoral art—whatever the brilliance and pathos in which it is clothed—is sooner or later condemned to destruction. Yet it would be a serious mistake to read into the preceding lines a demand for ethical tendentiousness or didacticism from art.

Art does not furnish evidence, neither does it provide a lesson—it presents emotions and transmits them from one heart to another. But there are emotions that are vacuous, insignificant, and even harmful. This must not to be forgotten in regard to the listener, and (most important) to oneself.

Art is at once consummation, incarnation, materialization and cannot, consequently, exist outside form and material. The greater degree to which such form and material are surmounted—even to the point of their almost ceasing to exist—the more easily and freely does the artist create, the more directly is his creative idea transmitted. Material is the instrument of creation, but not its aim and not its purpose. Whenever the observer's attention is captivated by material or form, it represents, more often than not, an obstacle to understanding. It is justified when the conscious purpose of the artist is to draw attention to internal by means of external imagery.

Emotionality may be directed mainly toward facts rather

than ideas. An idea transfigured by emotionality has already been transformed into feeling, which is to say, it has lost its abstract quality. Art does not tolerate the abstract or the rational, and that is why France is the nation poorest in emotional art—France, where rationality and abstraction reign, where generalization, with its tendency to unshakable canons, has built its nest.

Dealing as it does in the unrepeatable, the exceptional and the phenomenal, emotional art rejects rules, canons and generalities of every kind, recognizing as mandatory only the rules of a given artist for a given work. Consequently, every work of art may have its own style, its own tone and its own material. New or old, it makes no difference. It is essential to achieve action and to have feeling—that is all. Mastery or formal novelty devoid of emotional novelty is a trinket. All kinds of neologisms, of broken syntax—whatever you like—are possible, not for their own sake but for their unique expressiveness. But the poet's main task is to bring back to words their primitive purity and significance.

All epochs, all lands are accessible to art, but it focuses exclusively on the present. Past and future concern art only inasmuch as they are part of the present, or as the present renders them more sharply vivid. Retrospectivism—an attempt to present the past unrelated to the present—is an exercise devoid of life and utility; a created future, founded on data absent from the present, leads to senseless and to harmful utopias. Both are outside the realm of art, at least of emotive art. Such art is not archeology, and even though it admits the prophetic gift to be close to poetic creativity, it builds no utopias, envisaging future as clearly as present, heart to heart and eye to eye.

Life, fact, feeling and man—art always has these in its sights; but not concepts, not ideas, not rational constructions. Of course, logical constructions have their place in the process of creativity, but they are not the sources, not the basic elements of art. By means of intensity of individual emotion it is possible to make these basic elements mandatory; love of humanity can be made comprehensible through concrete love for an individual human being, but the reverse path, from the general to the individual, is unthinkable and destructive. Art cannot be ruled by the assumptions that somewhere exists (either eternally or provisionally) some kind of general laws concerning aesthetics, ethics and logic; art cannot derive from abstract preconceptions of humanity, duty, virtue, etc. It becomes devitalized and infertile, i.e.—not art. Emotionalism moves from the particular to the general, to the national and to the universal, not necessarily achieving its ultimate boundaries, but firmly convinced that for art this is the only possible way, expanding upwards rather than contracting downwards.

As source of our creativity and our vital essence, art cannot in any way be based on contradictory elements: material, form and mechanization. Comprised of motion and love, art will not tolerate anything immobile and unimpassioned. It is intolerant of all inflexible (even those provisionally so) rules, canons and formulae.

Schools founded on formalistic method cannot pretend to be artistic movements. They amount to disastrous distraction for idle, vacant individuals. It is good if one is in command of the devices of all existing schools, and capable of inventing new ones. Otherwise they may hinder or obstruct, like brats or puppies—and such is not what is required of them. Here the gift of inventiveness—which, after all, has nothing in common with the gift of creativity—may be appropriate.

The formal approach to art is suitable only for statistics and cataloguing, being unsuited even to criticism. It is impossible to understand, to experience or to feel (no matter if all three words be old-fashioned) a work of art solely by a description of its external features. A standpoint is called for, a predilection, a functioning of the emotions. To understand means either to love or to be horrified. To those who strive crassly to elucidate the inner motions of a living man, the mysterious intent of his emotional impulses, by means of a clockwork mechanism, the living man will prove to be a corpse, a wax doll. Art wields the power of a werewolf over those who deserve it. For a gravedigger any flowering mead is but a possible lot for a cemetery.

Art will slam the door in their faces. Describe it as much as you like, measure those closed shutters, but do not think that you are in any conceivable way dealing with art. But when formal study yields even the most feeble results, no more than a shadow of comprehension—it inevitably indicates that the critic has betrayed his method, deceiving either the reader or himself. Living people may be encountered (it's hard, but not impossible to imagine) among formalist critics whose attempts to make mannequins of themselves are not always crowned with success. In moments of weakness or revulsion against the meaningless and odious role they have adopted, they too can let slip a living word.

But schools whose practitioners characterize themselves with formal devices represent a species of monstrous incomprehension, of self-destruction.

Not only critics may be led into error by formal markings. Thus, Cézanne is included in a series of monographs on the German Expressionists (*Junge Kunst*), even though the new art of Germany is entirely opposed to him. Expressionism opposes itself not only to Futurism, Cubism and Impressionism but also to the culture of the nineteenth century in its entirety, founded, as it was, on positivism, materialism, the canon and mechanization. In this, and not yet in individual achievement, lie its power and its range. And Cézanne, that nineteenth-century Raphael with his dream of an unshakable canon, of texture, etc.—is the most unemotional, utterly abstract and generalizing of masters. Their absence of unity of method and device makes it possible to interpret the Expressionists as the heirs of Cubism and Futurism, thus depriving this unique movement of its meaning. This is because the meaning of it is to be located in the howl, the scream against mechanization, automation, dismemberment and disanimation of life, against the technological civilization that has led to war and to the horrors of capitalism—it is in the name of the soul, of humanity, of fact and the individual instance. A revolt against abstraction and ideology on the one hand, against crass deification on the other. A revolt against method and canon. What kind of continuation of Cubism is this—Cubism, deriving, bone of bone, flesh of flesh, from the entire mechanical pre-revolutionary culture. Formal methods can to such an extent coincide that even the Expressionists claim Cézanne as grandfather, when he is in fact their bitterest enemy. A recent example. It may well be that a few will detect something in common between the sets for the motion picture *The Cabinet of Dr. Caligari* and Vladimir Lebedev's constructions for *Supper of Jests*, while each is in fact directly opposed to the other. By no means all the successful decor for *Caligari* is emotional through and through, and neither is the movie in its entirety, but it sharply and painfully pierces your soul. The superb work of Vladimir

Lebedev represents the conquest of a purely technological problem and has a unique visual and intellectual impact of its own. From a purely formal point of view, perhaps there is something in common between the two.

The Expressionists have shifted the center of gravity, and this is their main achievement, and a colossal one it is.

1924

Notes

Notes

INTRODUCTION

1. Mikhail Kuzmin. *Wings: Prose and Poetry*. Translated and edited by Neil Granoien and Michael Green with preface by Vladimir Markov (Ann Arbor: Ardis, 1972).

2. John E. Malmstad. "Mikhail Kuzmin: A Chronicle of His Life and Times." Mikhail Kuzmin. *Sobranie stikhov*. München, 1978. Vol. III: 7–319. John E. Malmstad, Nikolay A. Bogomolov. *Mikhail Kuzmin: Iskusstvo, zhizn', epokha*. Moscow, 1996; —. *Mikhail Kuzmin: A Life in Art* (Cambridge, MA: Harvard University Press, 1999).

3. For an excerpt in English translation, see *Out of the Blue*. Edited by Kevin Moss. San Francisco, 1997: 124–26.

4. An entry from Kuzmin's diary dated March 17, 1920, leaves no doubt of a drastic change of attitude toward his former friend: "All the time it seems to me that this isn't life, these aren't people, rehearsals, streets but rather some kind of tedious Satanic game of words and shadows, shadows, shadows. Yusha Chicherin, formerly a real source of vital energy, is a bent shadow somewhere among them."

5. Mikhail Kuzmin. *Selected Prose and Poetry*. Edited and Translated by Michael Green (Ann Arbor: Ardis, 1980).

6. As early as 1906, Vyacheslav Ivanov—prophet unawares—had defined Kuzmin as a "living anachronism" in a poem of that title.

7. Since Kuzmin could no longer make a living in journalism, in the 'thirties he became increasingly dependent on translation. He worked on opera libretti: among them Verdi's *Don Carlo* and *Falstaff*, with Alban Berg's *Wozzeck* as a contemporary offering. To Kuzmin also belongs the standard Russian version of Apuleius' *Golden Ass*. It was Shakespeare, however, to whom, as a translator, Kuzmin paid the most profound homage. Of the comedies, he translated *Love's Labour's Lost*, *The Two Gentlemen of Verona*, *The Taming of the Shrew*, *Much Ado about Nothing*, *The Merry Wives of Windsor*, *The Tempest*. Of the tragedies—*King Lear*; together with Vladimir Morits he put both parts of *Henry IV* into Russian. The fascinating topic of Kuzmin the translator of Shakespeare still awaits its explorer.

8. *Dukhovnye stikhi*—a genre of sung narrative folk poetry telling of visions, quests, visitations.

POETRY

Abbreviations

N—*Nets*, First Book of Verse (Moscow, 1908)
CP—*Clay Pigeons*, Third Book of Verse (St. Petersburg, 1914)

OE—*Otherworldly Evenings* (Petrograd, 1921)
P—*Parabolas*, Poems 1921–1922 (St. Petersburg-Berlin, 1923)
TBI—*The Trout Breaks the Ice* (Leningrad, 1929)
U—uncollected poems

My Forebears (N)

d'Orsay and Brummel—Alfred Guillaume Gabriel d'Orsay (1801–52), George Bryan ("Beau") Brummel (1778–1840), famous nineteenth-century dandies.
Delightful actors of no great talent—maternal ancestor of Kuzmin, the French actor Jean Aufresne (1728–1804).
Mahomet—tragedy by Voltaire (1741).
Marcailhou—Marcailhou d'Emeric (1807–55), French composer of popular valses.
drama school blossoms—Kuzmin's mother, Nadezhda Dmitriyevna (née Fyodorova, 1834–1904), had been a student at the Imperial Drama School.

This Summer's Love (N)

Pavel Konstantinovich Maslov—Kuzmin's lover 1906–07, a young man of indeterminate occupation.

1. Where shall I find a style . . .

Marivaux—Pierre Carlet de Chamblain de Marivaux (1688–1763), French dramatist and novelist.

3. O lips kissed by so many . . .

Antinous—c.AD 110–30, favorite of the Emperor Hadrian (AD 76–138, ruled 117–38), drowned in the Nile. Hadrian deified him and established temples for his cult. Antinous is a recurring image in Kuzmin's work. "Antinous" also was a nickname given to Kuzmin by Lydia Zinov'yeva-Annibal (1866–1907), writer and wife of the poet Vyacheslav Ivanov. The couple's top floor apartment ("The Tower") housed St. Petersburg's most influential literary salon of the day, where Kuzmin was a vivid presence.
Thersites—a personage from Homer's *Iliad*; in the ancient world, embodiment of physical deformity and malice.

5. A parched rose drooped in doleful fashion . . .

that aria of Rosina . . . Pesaro's swan—Gioacchino Rossini (1792–1868) was born in the central Italian city of Pesaro. Rosina's aria "Io sono docile, sono rispettosa" is from the second act of *Il barbiere di Siviglia* (1816).

8. Every evening I look down from the steep . . .

The Kamensk one, the Volga one, or the Lyubim one—Kamensk and Lyubim—homeports of passing steamships; "Volga" here is the name of a shipping company.

Alexandrian Songs (N)

Kuzmin named as his sources for the "Alexandrian Songs" a translation of ancient Egyptian texts published by the English Society of Biblical Archaeology in the 1870s; the "Songs" also echo the *Chansons de Bilitis* of Pierre Louÿs (see below).
Feofilaktov Nikolai Petrovich (1878–1941)—artist and friend of Kuzmin (designed covers for *Wings* and *Nets*). An album of Feofilaktov's drawings (1909) bears the inscription, in English: "To Mr. Robert Ross the true devoted friend of Oscar Wilde a Russian admirer of his noble conduct towards one of England's greatest men. N. Théophilaktoff" (private collection).

I. *Prelude*

1. *Like a mother's lullaby . . .*

Cybele—Latin name of Greek Rhea, a fertility goddess.
Nike—Greek goddess of victory.

II. *Love*

7. *Were I a general of olden times . . .*

the tomb of Menkaure—Menkaure's is one of the three great pyramids at Ghiza, near Cairo.

III. *She*

2. *In spring the poplar renews its leaves . . .*

Adonis—beloved of Aphrodite, was destined by the verdict of Zeus to pass part of the year in the kingdom of the dead and part on earth with Aphrodite.

5. *In Imitation of Pierre Louÿs*

Pierre Louÿs (1870–1925), French writer, author of *Chansons de Bilitis* (1894), allegedly translated from the writings of Bilitis, a courtesan and poetess who lived in the sixth century BC. Oscar Wilde's *Salomé* is dedicated to Louÿs.

IV. *Wisdom*

2. *What's to be done . . .*

Callimachus (c.305–c.240 BC) Hellenistic poet, cataloguer of the Alexandrian Library.

4. Sweet is it to die . . .

Lucius *Apuleius* (second century AD) Roman writer, a favorite author of
Kuzmin, who provided the standard Russian translation of Apuleius'
novel *The Golden Ass.*

5. O sun, radiant one . . .

Ra—sun god in Egyptian mythology.
Helios—sun god in Greek mythology. The ancient Greeks identified Ra
with Helios.
Heliopolis—Biblical On, a city in Lower Egypt dedicated to the worship of
Ra.

V. Fragments

1. My son . . .

Ptah—god of the city of Memphis, demiurge who created both universe
and gods.
Isis—Egyptian goddess of fertility, water and wind; popular as a symbol of
femininity in the Hellenistic world. Isis plays an important role in Apuleius' *Golden Ass.*

2. When I was led through the gardens . . .

Hathor—Egyptian goddess of the sky, love, joy, music, and dance; the
Greeks identified her with Aphrodite.
sistra—percussion instrument, an attribute of Hathor.

3. What a downpour!

Tyrian dyer—Tyre, modern Lebanese Sour, ancient Phoenician city-state.

5. Three times I saw him face to face . . .

The poem describes several encounters with Antinous.
Lochias—imperial palace on the cape bordering the port of Alexandria.
Caesar—the Emperor Hadrian.
Nicomedia—town on the gulf of Izmit in the northwest of modern Turkey.

VI. Canopic Ditties

1. Life's light and free in Cánopus . . .

Cánopus—city on the coast of Lower Egypt in the Nile delta, connected by
a canal with ancient Alexandria. Cánopus was notorious for its orgies.

4. The Cyprian ranges in pursuit . . .

Cyprian—Aphrodite, who is associated with the island of Cyprus.

VII. Conclusion

Ephesus—Ionian city in W. Asia Minor.
Smyrna—modern Izmir, Turkey. Ancient Greek city on the western shore of Asia Minor.
Corinth—city of ancient Greece, on isthmus separating the Ionian and Aegean seas.

Quietly I take my leave of you . . .(CP)

The poem is addressed to Vsevolod Gavriilovich Knyazev (1891–1913), poet and lover of Kuzmin. Knyazev shot himself out of unrequited love for the actress Ol'ga Afanas'evna Glebova-Sudeikina (1885–1945; see notes to "And this is one for hooligans . . ." and "The Trout Breaks the Ice").
"How glorious is our God in Zion"—setting by Dmitrii Stepanovich Bortnyansky (1751–1825) of the anthem by Mikhail Matveyevich Kheraskov (1733–1807).
Tauride Gardens—a park in St. Petersburg.

Chodowiecki (OE)

Fuji in a Saucer (OE)

The Russian custom of drinking tea from a saucer is the basis of this poem. The poet observes the view of Mount Fuji decorating his saucer as he tips it to his mouth.

White Night (OE)

A seasonal absence of darkness is a natural phenomenon popularly associated with St. Petersburg.

Daniel Nikolaus Chodowiecki (1726–1801) German graphic artist and painter fond of depicting the everyday life of the German bourgeoisie.

Sophia. Gnostic Poems (1917–18) (OE)

Sophia is the personification of divine wisdom in both the Judaic and the Christian tradition. Sophia is allotted a key role in the system of Valentinus, a leading Gnostic philosopher of the second century. Sophia also has a central place in the system of Vladimir Sergeyevich Solov'yov (1853–1900, philosopher and poet).

Sophia

On the seven-columned throne—an image from the Proverbs of Solomon: "Wisdom hath builded her house, she hath hewn out her seven pillars" (Proverbs 9:1).

Basilides

Basilides—Gnostic philosopher of the second century. Like Valentinus, Basilides was an Alexandrian.

Aeon—a concept fundamental to Gnosticism; aeons are animated spheres, forming a world of eternal existence. Aeons range, in descending order of emanation, from the divine principle to the world of phenomena; the totality of aeons constitutes the *plenitude* of absolute existence—*Pleroma*.

" Αβραξαζ—"abraxas." Irenaeus of Lyons (c.130–c.202 AD) states that, according to Basilides, "abraxas" is the name of God (in Basilides' teaching, the Greek numerical equivalents of the word "abraxas" add up to 365—the totality of aeons).

Three issues of the literary journal *Abraksas* (1922–23) came out in Petrograd; Kuzmin took an active part in this venture.

Faustina

Annia Galeria Faustina (Faustina I, Empress, died AD 140/1), consort of the Emperor Antoninus Pius. After Faustina's death Antoninus built the temple to her memory by the Forum that is referred to in the poem.

Mentor

Bithynia—ancient land of Asia Minor, birthplace of Antinous.

Fish

Jewish fishermen—the brothers Andrew and Simon (Peter) summoned by Christ to be his disciples.

Hermes

In late antiquity Hermes assumed the features of Hermes Trismegistus ("thrice-great")—patron of the occult who guided the spirits of the dead to the underworld.

To the pure—all things are pure—from St. Paul's Epistle to Titus (Titus I:15).

Thrall (U)

This cycle was inspired by the arrest and imprisonment of Kuzmin's companion Yurii Ivanovich Yurkun in 1918. Yurkun (real name: Iosif Ivanovich Yurkunas, Lithuanian, 1895–1938) was seized during the wave of arrests with which the Bolsheviks responded to the assassination of Moisei Solomonovich Uritsky (1873–1918, chief of the Petrograd Cheka [secret police]) by Leonid Ioakimovich Kannegisser (1896–1918). Yurkun and Kuzmin were acquainted with Kannegisser, a Petrograd literary tyro, but neither of them was in any way involved in Uritsky's death. The assassination served as pretext for a "Red Terror"—the policy of seizing hostages from the "non-revolutionary" classes, followed by mass executions.

1. Angel of the Annunciation

Bearers of myrrh—the women who came to Christ's sepulcher to anoint his body (Mark 16:1–8; Luke 24:1–10).
Ezekiel's wheel—see Ezekiel 1:14–16
Tsarskoye—Tsarskoye selo (lit. "Tsar's Village"), town near St. Petersburg, before the Revolution a court residence of the imperial family.
Arakcheyev—Count Aleksei Andreyevich Arakcheyev (1769–1834)—between 1810 and 1825 Chairman of the Department of Military Affairs under Alexander I. During the last decade of Alexander's reign Arakcheyev enjoyed unlimited power, becoming notorious for his introduction of "military settlements," where deportees lived under an inhumane regime. Arakcheyev's name became a synonym for state-wielded terror.
"Albert's"—restaurant popular with St. Petersburg bohemians, officially the "Frantsuzskii" ("French"), 18 Nevsky Avenue, known by the name of its proprietor (see notes to "And this is one for hooligans . . .").
pricking of wine's needles—self-quotation. "Wine's Needles," cycle and poem in *The Guide* (Petersburg, 1918).
"Honi soit qui mal y pense"—"Evil be to him that thinks it," motto of the British Order of the Garter.

2. To Eyes that Meet

Secrets of New York, Mamzelle Zaza—names of popular movies.
Kolchak, the Siberian admiral—Aleksandr Vasil'evich Kolchak (1874–1920), appointed admiral in 1917. One of the leaders of anti-Bolshevik resistance, in 1918 proclaimed Supreme Commander, then Absolute Ruler of Russia. Parts of Siberia and the Far East were under Kolchak's control. Captured and shot by the Bolsheviks.

3. Floods

Monday Pure—in the calendar of the Orthodox Church, the first Monday of Great Lent, preceding Easter.

4. Lullaby

Naval barracks—*Morskiye kazarmy*—Yurkun was imprisoned here in the fall of 1918.
Mist behind Bars—lost novel by Yurkun, most likely inspired by his incarceration.
"Schlafe, mein Prinzchen, schlaf ein"—opening line of a lullaby by Mozart.

O otherworldly evenings . . . (OE)

This poem of 1919 opens a collection bearing the same title, published in 1921.

December frosts the rosy sky . . . (U)

This poem is one of the numerous examples of Kuzmin's responsiveness to the visual arts. "And we, like Menshikov in Beryozov, / We read the Bible and we wait" evokes a historical canvass by Vasilii Ivanovich Surikov (1848–1916), *Menshikov in Beryozov* (1883, Tretyakov Gallery, Moscow). The wide popularity of Surikov in Russia can scarcely be exaggerated; many of his paintings' titles have become proverbial.

Surikov's painting depicts Peter the Great's favorite, Aleksandr Daniilovich Menshikov (1673–1729), a stable-man's son who gained the titles of count, prince and generalissimo. At the summit of his career, under Peter, Menshikov accumulated legendary power and wealth. After the deaths of Peter and his successor Catherine I, Menshikov, now out of favor, was exiled to the Siberian village of Beryozov (now the town of Beryozovo in the Tyumen region).

Surikov pictures Menshikov, a man of towering stature, seated in a low-ceilinged peasant hut with two daughters and a son. One of the daughters is reading from a large open book (presumably the Bible) that lies before her. Menshikov and his children are warmly dressed: the hut is cold (cf. *Black the rooms of this unheated house*).

There is no talk of Wrangel now—Baron Pyotr Nikolayevich Wrangel (1878–1928), last Commander-in-Chief of the anti-Bolshevik Volunteer Army.

On the golden archangel alone / The sunbeams drowse delectably—St. Petersburg's skyline is dominated by the figure of a gilded archangel atop the belfry of SS Peter and Paul Cathedral (early eighteenth century, architect Dominico Trezzini).

Lost enchantment . . . (U)

"But the Admiralty is keen / To pierce the cerulean lees"—the Admiralty, with its famous needle, is at the center of the architectural complex of St. Petersburg, marking the confluence of the city's three main highways.

Not bitter to me . . . (U)

To fling into space . . . (P)

As girls dream of their fiancés . . . (P)

Catherine is betrothed to Christ—Catherine of Alexandria, martyr. According to one legend, Catherine was betrothed to Christ in a dream.

"And this one is for hooligans . . ." (P)

The poem is dedicated to Ol'ga Glebova-Sudeikina (see notes to "Quietly I take my leave of you . . ."), singer of the poem's leitmotif folksong, among whose listeners are:
A novelist, a poet, a composer—Yurkun, Kuzmin and Artur Sergeyevich Lourié (1892–1966).
Sounds of Kitezh—The tale of City of Kitezh is a central myth of Russian folklore: besieged by the Mongols, Kitezh sank into the earth in answer to the prayers of its inhabitants. Where the city had stood appeared the lake of Svetloyar (Nizhny Novgorod region)—a popular place of pilgrimage. According to tradition, the climax of such a pilgrim's spiritual quest is an ability to hear the ringing of the submerged city's bells. "The sounds of

Kitezh" may be connected with the opera *The Legend of the Invisible City of Kitezh and the Maiden Fevronia* (1904) by Nikolai Rimsky-Korsakov (1844–1908), Kuzmin's teacher at the St. Petersburg Conservatoire.

Pechora—river in NE Russia, on the bank of which stood Pustozyorsk, an Old-Believer sanctuary.

Karelian Konevetz—Rozhdestvensky Monastery, situated on Konevetz Island on Lake Ladoga (SW Karelia-N St. Petersburg region).

deep-blue Sarov—Sarovskaya Pustyn'. A hermitage in Tambov province, founded by *starets* ("elder") Seraphim of Sarov (1760–1833). Seraphim was the last saint to be canonized by the Russian Orthodox Church before the Revolution.

When this tide / Weakens, / A new one . . . Flows inexhaustibly—here again Kuzmin turns to a favorite theme: Russian sectarianism, persecuted by both church and state.

Police won't make it to the Vyg—river of Olonets and Archangel provinces, on the banks of which stood Vygoretskaya Pustyn', an Old-Believer stronghold.

Podpolniks, Khlysts and Beguns—various sects (literally "undergrounders," "flagellants" and "runaways").

And on far-floating islands living graves—the reference is to the sectarian practice of self-internment.

"If I forget Thee?"—see Psalm 137 (136 in the Russian Bible): "4. How shall we sing the Lord's song in a strange land? 5. If I forget thee, O Jerusalem, let my right hand forget her cunning." The rhetorical use to which Kuzmin puts this phrase requires a question mark missing from the biblical original.

"All Petersburg"—an annual directory, a kind of "Yellow Pages," of pre-revolutionary St. Petersburg. It would have reminded the city's denizens, particularly during the Civil War and "War Communism," of past diversity and abundance.

For 1913, say—1913 was the year in which the Romanov dynasty celebrated its tercentenary.

Fairs . . . there they are / In Nizhny—the annual fair of Nizhny Novgorod, a pan-Russian commercial enterprise, ceased to exist under Soviet rule.

Stenka's rock—an ironic reference to a popular song *Yest' na Volge utyos . . .* ("On the Volga there's a rock . . ."), which might have provided the conventional dweller in the capital with a simplistic notion of Russian provincial life. Sten'ka (Stepan) Razin, leader of a Cossack uprising (1667–71), became a hero of folksong.

"Albert's"—see notes to "Thrall" (1. Angel of the Annunciation).

No governor's lady with officer conversing (U)

First published in 1987 in the Paris-based *Russkaya mysl'* by Gennady Shmakov (a pioneer Kuzmin scholar, 1940–88).

Devoid of name a country cannot be. / There is no salvation in initials alone. Kuzmin alludes here to the initials that form Russia's new, Bolshevik-imposed name: R.S.F.S.R—Russian Soviet Federal Socialist Republic.

Fourteenth of December

This was the date, in 1825, of an attempted coup d'état organized by a number of high-ranking military aristocrats (the "Decembrist Revolt"). The uprising took place on St. Petersburg's Senate Square.

Pugachov—Yemel'yan Pugachov (1742–75), leader of a Cossack revolt (1773–75), claiming to be Emperor Peter III (reigned 1761–62), who had been assassinated in the military coup that established his consort as Empress Catherine II ("the Great").

Sand—the German student Karl Sand in 1819 assassinated August von Kotzebue (b. 1761), the popular German dramatist who was also a Russian civil servant. Sand was rightly convinced that Kotzebue was spying for Russia.

The Trout Breaks the Ice

The collection *Forel' razbivayet led* (*The Trout Breaks the Ice*) was published in 1929 by *Izdatel'stvo pisatelei* ("Writers' Publishing House"), Leningrad. *Trout* was the last collection published during the poet's lifetime.
The cycle is dedicated to Anna Dmitriyevna Radlova (1891–1949)—a poet much admired by Kuzmin, and an ally in his attempt to launch Emotionalism (see "Literary Manifestoes").

Second Prologue

painter long sea-slain—Nikolai Nikolayevich Sapunov (1880–1912), painter, designer for Komissarzhevskaya's theater. Kuzmin witnessed Sapunov's drowning, recollections of which haunted him for the rest of his life.
a hussar, a stripling, / With a bullet through his brain . . . —Vsevolod Knyazev (see notes to "Quietly I take my leave of you . . ."). Knyazev was an officer in the Sixteenth Irkutsk Hussar Regiment, stationed in Riga.
Mister Dorian—the nickname of the "eternally youthful" Yurkun.

Kuzmin's diary, under the date August 14, 1926, describes a nightmare obviously linked with this poem:

> Yesterday a terrible dream. A room, big and new but very isolated—nothing to be heard either from outside or inside. I am alone. But the silence is full of sounds. The doors are terribly small and distant. Music. Suddenly a swarm of mice and the ballet buff Litovkin, a suicide, as a Lilliputian; he plays the flute and the mice dance. I look on with interest and a certain amount of fear. A knock at the door. The mice have disappeared. Hardly anyone comes to visit us. A guest. A stranger, but I vaguely remember something. The usual formula: "You don't recognize me—we have met somewhere or other." Another knock. "That's probably Sapunov," he says. Horror. It really is Sapunov. Yur. [Yurkun] by some miracle is here already. Nikolai Nikolayevich [Sapunov] the same as he used to be, only older and a bit swollen. In absolute horror I make the sign of the cross over him: "May God rise from the dead" and the "Lord's Prayer." He screws up his face in anger: "So that's the way you meet old friends, Miguel?" "That's all I need, all kinds of cadavers dragging themselves to see me!" It's perfectly clear to me now that the first one is also deceased. Yur. intervenes: "What's the matter, Michel? The body of Nikolai Nikolayevich [Sapunov] was never found—he might well be alive." "So why are you afraid of the cross?" "Time to put a stop to this humbug. Isn't any pleasure in it." I calm down, overcome my revulsion and kiss the stone-cold Sapunov, introduce him to Yur. We seat ourselves on the sofa like real guests. We all flop down. Then on top of everything else, in the heat of an argument he offers me a thousand rubles. Drags out a wad of banknotes. I remember that if you dream of someone dead, you should neither take anything from him nor give anything to him, so I refuse. He understands what I am thinking, screws up his face and hides the money. "All right, it's up to you." A new guest. Definitely one of the deceased.

Some sort of musician, rather a cutie. They are all ill-shaven, a bit dirty, their clothes are wrinkled, but it's obvious that even primitive propriety such as this costs them enormous effort to maintain. They are all menacing and vengeful. In Sapunov there is a vague goodwill toward me, remote as if it came up from the bottom of the sea (and yet he is the most vindictive of the three). Inquiries about friends. "Yes, we heard from so-and-so and so-and-so (recently deceased)." The way they talk there, the way they bear malice, the way they lure us in. "You are highly valued there." As if it were a foreign country. Posthumous fame—and while I am still alive. They prepare to leave. "We've had a lovely time. Nice to recall the old days. Half-a-dozen spots are all that are left where it's possible to get together." O my God, they'll be calling on me! I step outside to see them off. Somebody says on the landing: "So they're haunting you too now. It's that kind of apartment—nobody even lives there." I don't remember whether or not they drank or ate. Smoke they certainly did. Could it be a picture of our life, or is it an omen?

Thrust the First

"Tristan"—Richard Wagner's opera *Tristan und Isolde* (1865).
A beauty from a painting by Bryullov—Karl Bryullov (1799–1852)—Russian artist, the fashionable portraitist of his generation.

Thrust the Second

"Maritza, whoa!"—refrain of concluding aria from *Countess Maritza*, operetta by Imre Kalman (1924).

Thrust the Third

Shakespeare . . . "The Sonnets"—Kuzmin was working on a translation of the sonnets in the 1930s. It has not survived.

Thrust the Fifth

Greenock—Scottish port to the west of Glasgow.

Thrust the Tenth

"Caligari!"—Robert Wiene's silent movie *Das Kabinett des Dr. Caligari* (1919) made a profound impression on Kuzmin.

Thrust the Twelfth

On the bridge the horses glisten—reference here is to four sculptured equine groups, each with an equerry. Sculpted by Baron Pyotr Klodt in 1841, these groups adorn the Anichkov Bridge over the Fontanka river crossing Nevsky Avenue, St. Petersburg's main thoroughfare.

In Memoriam Lydia Ivanova (U)

Lydia Ivanova (1903–24) Petrograd ballerina who drowned in mysterious circumstances (there were rumors of the Cheka's involvement in a supposed accident). Ivanova's death became part of the city's literary mythology.

Were I a painter, I would paint . . . (U)

Ol'ga Aleksandrovna Cheremshanova (1904–70) poet, to a collection of whose verse Kuzmin wrote an introduction.

Settlers (U)

This poem has survived thanks only to the literary scholar and translator Ivan Alekseyevich Likhachev (1902–72), who preserved it in his memory throughout years in prison and concentration camp.
John E. Malmstad and Vladimir Markov, the editors of a pioneering three volume collection of Kuzmin's work point out in their commentary that "Settlers'" American setting was suggested by "a few pages in Dickens's *Martin Chuzzlewit.*"

THEATER

THE DEATH OF NERO

Nero was given its impetus by the death and funeral of Vladimir Lenin in 1924. An entry from Kuzmin's diary dated January 28, 1924:

> After the funeral the weather quieted and became milder: all the devils calmed down. What a hodgepodge of lies and charlatanism these speeches all are. Not so much an "epidemic of insanity" as one of crookedness, one that has assumed a scale that makes it possible to mistake it for insanity. But does not its very scale amount to a confirmation? The whole world dragged through drunken vomit— such is the world order of Communism. [. . .] Had the idea of writing a *Death of Nero.*

Sergei Ernestovich Radlov (1892–1958) director, husband of Anna Dmitriyevna Radlova (see notes to "The Trout Breaks the Ice"); was a co-signer of "Declaration of Emotionalism."

Act One

1ˢᵗ Tableau

Pavel Andreyevich Lukin—Kuzmin often endows his characters with "telling" names; the fact that name, patronymic and family name of a protagonist who is writing a play about Nero echoes the names of three apostles (Paul, Andrew, Luke), can hardly be accidental, taking account of the drama's "evangelical" parallelism. The heroine's name—Marie, a French-based diminutive for Maria Petrovna Rublyova—apart from its most obvious echo (Marie-Mary) has another significant one: Andrei Rublyov— supreme master of medieval Russian religious painting (c.1360/70–1430).

3ʳᵈ Tableau

Nero—Lucius Domitius Ahenobarbus (AD 37–68) ruled as Nero, Emperor of Rome (AD 54–68). Nero was son of *Agrippina* the Younger (AD 15–59).

Her third husband was her uncle, the Emperor *Claudius* (10 BC–AD 54, ruled 41–54). Agrippina poisoned Claudius to secure the succession of Nero.

7ᵗʰ Tableau

There are lots of gingerheads in our family, that's why we're "Enobarbi."— Much of Kuzmin's historical data is taken from Suetonius' *Lives of the Twelve Caesars*. Suetonius recounts a legend, according to which the progenitor of the Ahenobarbi, Lucius Domitius, encountered celestial youths whose touch turned his beard from black to ruddy.

Act Two

1ˢᵗ Tableau

Seneca—Lucius Annaeus Seneca, the Younger (4 BC–AD 65), tragedian and Stoic philosopher, Roman senator, tutor to Nero, on whose orders he committed suicide.

4ᵗʰ Tableau

"My plans are known to you: everything is calculated to be spread over a four-year period"—the first Five Year Plan was imposed on Soviet Russia in 1928.
Tyukhe—τύχη, "chance" in Greek. Suetonius mentions Nero's possession of an "image of a girl," which he worshiped.

5ᵗʰ Tableau

"Stenka Razin"—the folksong *"Iz-za ostrova na strezhen'"* . . . ("Past the island, toward the deep . . .") was inspired by Stenka, leader of a Cossack revolt (see notes to "And this one is for hooligans . . .").
La belle Hélène—operetta by Jacques Offenbach (1864).

10ᵗʰ Tableau

Atellan—derived from Atella, ancient Oscan town (now Atella di Napoli, seven miles north of Naples) famed as the cradle of early Roman farce.
Datus . . . Isidorus the Cynic—according to Suetonius, Datus represented in his pantomime drinking and swimming—reference to the fates of Claudius and Agrippina. Toward the end of his performance Datus indicated the senate by a gesture. Both Datus and Isidorus were to be banished from Rome for their irreverence toward Nero.
Vindex—Gaius Julius Vindex raised the first, unsuccessful, revolt against Nero in AD 68.
"Kill the Christians and save Rome!"—adaptation of the notorious rallying

cry of ultra-nationalist, anti-Semitic organizations and groups in pre-revolutionary Russia "Kill the yids and save Russia!"

Act Three

2nd Tableau

Locusta—poisoner who put her skill to the service of both Agrippina and Nero.

3rd Tableau

LSPO—John E. Malmstad and Vladimir Markov, the drama's first editors, decipher these initials as *Leningradskii soyuz potrebitel'skikh obshchestv* (Leningrad Union of Consumer Societies). There is an apparently deliberate merging here of the *realia* of Pavel's madhouse with those of late 1920's Leningrad (cf. Kuzmin's observation concerning "barbaric names of various [Soviet] institutions" in "Underground Streams").

4th Tableau

Galba—Servius Sulpicius Galba (3 BC–AD 69), Emperor AD 68–69.

6th Tableau

Icelus did promise, didn't he?—Nero's request that his body be buried unmutilated was granted by Icelus Marcianus (Galba's freedman and counselor).

PROSE

"HIGH ART"

The story was first published in the almanac *Grekh* ("Sin," Moscow, 1911: 76–100), without the dedication that was added when the story was republished in M. Kuzmin, *Tret'ya kniga rasskazov* Moscow, 1913: 105–41. *Nikolai Stepanovich Gumilev* (1886–1921) poet and dramatist, founder of the post-Symbolist poetic school of Acmeism. Both Kuzmin and Gumilev contributed to the St. Petersburg journal *Apollo*.

The female protagonist of "High Art," Zoya Gorbunova caricatures Zinaida Nikolayevna Gippius (1869–1945), a prominent representative of *starshii simvolizm* (the "senior [generation of] Symbolism"). Gippius was opposed to Kuzmin's writings no less than she was to Gumilev's (her reaction to *Wings* was dismissive; the caricature of Gumilev as one Gushchin in her drama *Makov tsvet* ["The Red Poppy," 1908] is unsparing, even down to the young poet's speech defect). Turning Gippius's own weapon against her (encoding the family name of a prototype in that of a character, cf. *Gumilev / Gushchin*), Kuzmin mocks Gippius as a literary grandstander.

The story also alludes to a hoax connected with the poet Cherubina de

Gabriak (pseudonym of Elizaveta Ivanonvna Dmitrieyeva, 1887–1928), of whom—exclusively by mail—were enamored virtually the entire editorial board of *Apollo*. Among the stricken were Gumilev and the editor-in-chief of *Apollo* Sergei Konstantinovich Makovsky (1877–1962). The "mysterious poetess," supposedly a Spanish aristocrat and a devout Catholic, was revealed to be a Russian woman with a Russian name, and the perpetrator of the prank to be the poet Maksimilian Aleksandrovich Voloshin (1877–1932). What was intended as a joke led to a duel between Gumilev and Voloshin (November 22, 1909), which happily left both participants—and Russian literature—unscathed. One of Voloshin's seconds was the novelist Aleksei N. Tolstoy (1882–1945), one of Gumilev's—Mikhail Kuzmin.

"beaver collar was silvered with frostdust"—cited from Pushkin's *Eugene Onegin*, Chapter One, XVI.
Zoya Nikolayevna Gorbunova—the initials of the entire name, the patronymic as a whole, coincide with those of Zinaida Nikolayevna Gippius.
This was a time when mysterious poetesses had yet to came into vogue—before there was such an abundance of literary lionesses—a hint at the Cherubina de Gabriak affair.
Sergei Auslender—Sergei Abramovich Auslender (1886–1943), writer and dramatist, Kuzmin's nephew.
the words of St. Ephraim the Syrian—the prayer of St. Ephraim (c.306–73) is another Pushkinian echo (see Pushkin's poem *Otsy pustynniki i zhyony neporochny* ["Hermit monks and blameless women ..."], 1836).

UNDERGROUND STREAMS

Novaya Rossiya 2 (1922): 23–28.
Merezhkovsky—Dmitrii Sergeyevich Merezhkovsky (1865–1941), writer and philosopher, husband of Zinaida Gippius. Both emigrated after the Revolution to the West, where they took an extreme anti-Bolshevik stance.
For all his idyllic surname, Maksim Ivanovich Krylechkin ...—an idyllic tone is suggested by the character's folksy-sounding family name (derived from *kryl'tso*—porch of a dwelling), with the diminutive suffix "chk."
The Journey of Young Kostis—a book of this title was published by a Masonic propagator of the Enlightenment in Russia, Nikolai Novikov (1744–1818).
Khlebnikov—Velimir Khlebnikov (real name and patronymic: Viktor Vladimirovich, 1885–1922)—poet, dramatist and theoretician of Russian Futurism.
Aleksei Mikhailovich is terribly homesick—name and patronymic are identical to those of Aleksei Mikhailovich Remizov, émigré writer who was to die in Paris (see notes to "Concerning Beautiful Clarity").

LITERARY MANIFESTOES

CONCERNING BEAUTIFUL CLARITY

Apollo 4 (1910): 5–10.
a humdrum Moscow anecdote—in all likelihood, directed at the writings of Andrei Bely (pseudonym of Boris Nikolayevich Bugayev, 1880–1934).

Le bourgeois gentilhomme—Kuzmin quotes, slightly inaccurately, Act 2, scene 4 (not 6) of Molière's comedy.

Ostrovsky—Aleksandr Nikolayevich Ostrovsky (1823–86), dramatist known for his depiction of Russian bourgeois mores.

Pechersky—Andrei Pechersky (pseudonym of Pavel Ivanovich Mel'nikov, 1818–83). As an official attached to the Niznhy Novgorod provincial administration, and later to the Ministry of Internal Affairs, Mel'nikov was responsible for surveillance of the Old Believers. Mel'nikov's knowledge of the sectarians' way of life is reflected in his four-volume epic *V lesakh, Na gorakh* ("In the Forests," "In the Mountains," 1871–81). Mel'nikov's influence is discernable in Kuzmin's *Wings*.

Leskov—Nikolai Semyonovich Leskov (1831–95), writer celebrated for his mastery of Russian folk idiom.

Dahl's Dictionary—Vladimir Ivanovich Dahl (1801–72), writer, lexicographer, ethnographer. Dahl devoted his life to work on *Tolkovyi slovar' zhivogo velikorusskogo yazyka* ("Reasoned Dictionary of the Living Great-Russian Language," published 1863–66). Dahl's dictionary remains the classic work of its kind in Russian.

"The Queen of Spades," "Scenes from Medieval Times," the fragment "Caesar was journeying . . ."—all by Pushkin. "The Queen of Spades"—c. 1833; "Scenes from Medieval Times" or "Scenes from the Age of Chivalry"—unfinished and untitled sketch, dated August 15, 1835; "Caesar was journeying . . ."—narrative fragment that takes its name from its opening words (also known as "Scenes from Roman Life"), 1833, 1835.

Song of Triumphant Love—a late work by Ivan Turgenev (1881), dedicated to the memory of Gustave Flaubert.

Leskov's legends—a group of stories based on ancient Russian saints' lives and didactic tales (*Skomorokh Pamfolon* ["Pamfolon the Jester," 1887], *Prekrasnaya Aza* ["Beautiful Aza," 1888], etc.), which influenced Kuzmin's prose.

Bryusov's Fiery Angel—novel by Valerii Bryusov set in the sixteenth century (1908).

Auslender—see notes to "High Art."

Remizov's Leimonarion—an attempt (1907) by Aleksei Mikhailovich Remizov (1877–1957, see notes to "Underground Streams") to revive ancient folk speech and the genre of the saint's life ("Leimonarion"—"The Spiritual Meadow"—is the name of John Moschus' [c.AD 600] compilation of sayings and stories from the early fathers of Egypt and Sinai).

Declaration of Emotionalism

Abraksas [3] (February) [Petrograd] (1923): 3.

This manifesto was Kuzmin's first attempt at proclaiming a new literary movement, one that was modeled on German Expressionism. "Declaration of Emotionalism," composed by Kuzmin, was signed by Anna and Sergei Radlov and Yurii Yurkun.

Emotionality as a Basic Element of Art

Arena. Petersburg (1924): 9–12.

Vladimir Lebedev—theater designer Vladimir Vasil'evich Lebedev (1891–1967).

The Supper of Jests—*La cena delle beffe* (1909), play by Sem Benelli (Italian, 1877–1949).